25 Ski Tours in the Adirondacks

25 Ski Tours in the Adirondacks

BY ALMY AND ANNE COGGESHALL

New Hampshire Publishing Company   Somersworth

Acknowledgments

This book would not have been possible without the help and cooperation of a number of individuals. We would particularly like to acknowledge the assistance of William M. White, Theodore Feurer, Raymond Falacz, Robert Moore, and James Spring of Schenectady; James Wright and Peter Bleau of Turin; James Chauftey and Robert Berry of the staff of the Whetstone Gulf State Park; Benjamin P. Coe of the Tug Hill Commission; and Livingston Lansing, Vincent J. Schaefer, and Austin Hogan of the Atmospheric Sciences Research Center, State University of New York.

An Invitation to the Reader

Occasionally trails are rerouted and signs and landmarks altered. If you find that changes have occurred on the routes described in this book, please let the authors and publisher know so that corrections may be made in future editions. Other comments and suggestions are also welcome. Address all correspondence:

Editor, *Ski Tours*
New Hampshire Publishing Company
Box 70
Somersworth, NH 03978

International Standard Book Number: 0-89725-008-7
Library of Congress Catalog Card Number: 79-88594

Published by New Hampshire Publishing Company
Somersworth, New Hampshire 03878

Printed in the United States of America
Design by Uneeda Design, Inc.

Photograph on page 16 by Vincent J. Schaefer; photographs on pages 63 and 78 by Ted Feurer; back cover photograph by Martha D'Ambrosio; all other photographs by the authors.

Dedication

John S. Apperson (1881-1963)

This book is dedicated to the memory of John S. Apperson, who pioneered ski touring, skate sailing, and winter camping in New York around the turn of the century. His untiring efforts to protect and enlarge the New York State Forest Preserve contributed to this magnificent land being preserved for the benefit of future generations.

He was the first to climb the major Adirondack summits on skis. The picture shows him on Mount Marcy in 1914.

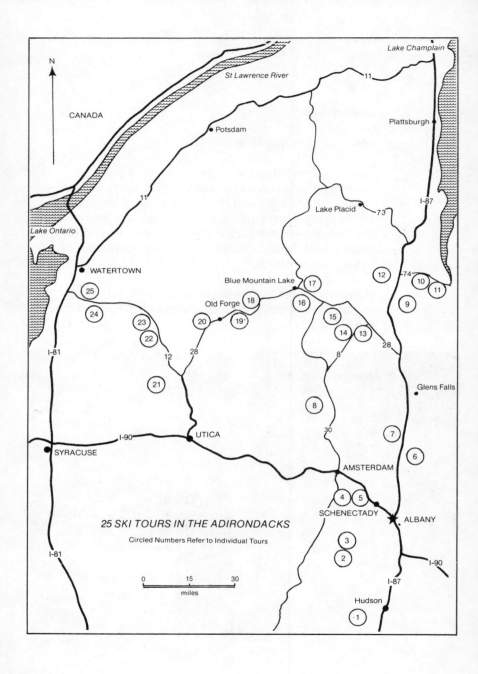

25 SKI TOURS IN THE ADIRONDACKS

Circled Numbers Refer to Individual Tours

Contents

Introduction

Welcome to New York! Welcome to the spectacular
scenery you'll discover in the Empire State. Welcome
particularly to the diversity of ski touring opportunities you'll find in this part of the snowbelt.

The next few pages will acquaint you with this book.
Here you will learn how the twenty-five tours are
arranged into five principal groups, with each group
being clustered around towns or villages that can serve
as a weekend headquarters. You will learn about the
New York State Forest Preserve and about its legally
designated wilderness areas and the unique kind of
skiing they provide. You will find information on
outdoor living and winter survival. Suggestions are
included on how to keep your car functioning in the
New York winters. And, since skiing is a weather
dependent activity, there is a snowfall map for the state
to help you plan your trips and a special section on the
furious storms that blow in from Lake Ontario and the
tremendous accumulations they produce. Parts of
western New York receive more snow than any other
part of the United States east of the Rocky Mountains.
Finally, there is a brief section on how to use the book.

The most important part of this guide is, of course, the
tours themselves. In addition to detailed descriptions
of the actual trails that we recommend, we have
attempted to draw in threads of local history and to
mention the influence of important people or
significant events. There is not a spot in New York that
does not have some tale to tell if you only search it out.
We hope that these touches of local color will add to
your enjoyment and to your appreciation of these areas.

Something for Everyone

We have tried to provide for a wide range of Nordic
skiing opportunities. All these tours are on land open
to the public, so no trail fees are involved. Some are in
state or national parks, where trails are sometimes
packed or groomed. At the other extreme are long
penetrations into remote wilderness areas where you
are entirely on your own. Some routes are essentially
level; others have challenging downhill runs. In
addition, we have noted when ski touring centers are
close to these routes so that you can combine the best
of both worlds in a weekend outing.

In this book we have chosen to emphasize the remote
and backwoods type of ski touring opportunities. We
wished to be a voice that would speak for the quiet
places in the state. Our book is directed to those who
have learned the sport in the resort context and now
want to move to more private and more personally
challenging experiences.

How the Tours are Arranged

The geographical distribution of the tours is shown on
the location map facing the table of contents. Starting
with Tour 1 on the line of cliffs near Catskill, Tours 1
through 8 are generally central to Albany. You will
reach the jumping-off place for Tours 9 through 12 by
taking I-87 to Schroon Lake. Tours 13 through 17 are
near the eastern end of NY 28, which you can easily
reach if you base yourself in Warrensburg, North
Creek, or Indian Lake. Tours 18, 19, and 20 are
convenient to Old Forge, Inlet, and Eagle Bay, all close
together on the western end of NY 28. Tours 21
through 25 are in or near the Tug Hill Plateau, with
easy access from Boonville or Lowville on NY 12.

New York State's "Forever Wild"

Fourteen of our tours are located on lands of the New York State Forest Preserve, and nine of these are in legally designated wilderness areas. In these areas you will be skiing through forests, which although not strictly pristine, are among the closest you can come to authentic wilderness conditions anywhere east of the Mississippi River.*

Reacting to the abuses of the logging industry during the nineteenth century, the New York State Constitutional Convention of 1894 enacted an amendment to the state constitution that has had far-reaching effects. The first legislation of its kind, it was designed to protect and preserve certain state lands in a wild and natural state. This protection applies to state lands only, not to private holdings in the same areas. The land thus safeguarded is called the Forest Preserve. The protection is conveyed in these historic words:

"The lands of the State, now owned or hereafter acquired, constituting the Forest Preserve as now fixed by law shall forever be kept as wild forest lands. They shall not be leased, sold or exchanged, nor taken by any corporation, public or private, and the timber thereon shall not be sold, removed or destroyed."

This pioneering legislation was far ahead of its time. Seventy years later, it influenced the development of the Federal Wilderness Act of 1964. In 1972 New York's Forest Preserve lands were additionally classified as wilderness, primitive, and wild forest. Lands classified

*There is an area of undisturbed virgin forest in the Five Ponds Wilderness Area south and southwest of Cranberry Lake between Sand Lake and the Five Ponds in the northern Adirondacks. (See USGS 15' Cranberry Lake.)

as wilderness are to be administered according to
standards almost identical to those that apply to
Federal wilderness areas. Greater latitude is given to
nonconforming uses on lands under the other two
classifications. This is why you will find snowmobile
trails and jeep roads on wild forest lands but not in the
official wilderness areas.

In the past wild and formidable territory maintained
its own defenses against man-made intrusions. Today
the power of modern technology is such that these
natural defenses have lost their effectiveness. Because
our growing population, expanding settlements, and
increasing mechanization threaten to occupy and
modify all parts of the country, leaving none in a
natural state, it is considered in the public interest to
create a system of wilderness lands.

When you are skiing in such territory, you cannot
expect to encounter the same values found at
conventional ski resorts. At resorts the land has been
modified to optimize your skiing experience. The trails
are designed for the best width, grades, and curves.
The tracks are groomed. And a full-service resort
invariably has warming rooms, pro shops, instruction,
and accommodations.

In land managed as wilderness, the inverse applies.
The user is expected to adapt himself to Nature's
conditions, not the other way around. While you may
come across a track made by a previous skier, you
must take the snow the way you find it. The trails may
be narrow. There may be locally steep spots. The
stream crossings may or may not be bridged. The
motivation to enter such areas must include a thirst
for adventure, for the unexpected, for natural beauty,
and for unspoiled conditions. The wilderness demands
skiing skill as well as a reserve of stamina. Even more

important is proficiency in the pioneer arts of
backwoods navigation, map reading, snow and ice
craft, fire-building, self-rescue, and other outdoor
living skills. The rewards are in a greater sense of
privacy and isolation and in developing your own
sense of independence and self-reliance. You can also
expect a total absence of motorized vehicles.

About Litter

So much has been written along the lines of "if you
carry it in, please carry it out" and "leave nothing but
footprints" that it hardly seems necessary to ask that
you leave nothing behind that will show up the following spring to disfigure the spots where you have
been. This includes lunch papers, ski wax wrappers,
film cartons, and beverage containers. A plastic bag
will hold all these residues. Please take them home too.
Don't drop your litter bag in the parking lot.

Your Winter Survival Kit

People often ask us what they should take with them
in case something happens and they're caught out in
the woods overnight. We would like to tell you about a
forest ranger we know whose duties require that he be
ready to strike off in the backcountry on searches for
lost persons in any season and in any weather.

He carries a small day pack that contains a reflective
waterproof tarp, two small pieces of closed-cell
insulating foam, a large plastic bag, a small pot to melt
snow or to brew hot drinks, and enough cold rations to
last him through supper, breakfast, and lunch. He
always has a thick wool hat and extra clothing suited
to the season.

If he has to spend the night in the woods, he looks for a spot out of the wind. He dresses warmly, puts his feet in the plastic bag, sits down on one piece of the insulating foam, and puts the other under his feet. The center of the reflective waterproof tarp goes over his head so that all four sides drape on the ground. He curls up with his head on his arms, puts his arms on his knees, and spends the night in this heat-conserving position.

All the foregoing stows in little space. Survival considerations aside, the insulating foam makes a fine sit-upon, the tarp can serve as a wind-screen during lunch, while the plastic bag keeps your feet warm. This kit has such general-purpose utility that you should assemble one and carry it at all times. It almost goes without saying that you should always carry matches, a compass, and a map.

To Forestall Emergencies

- Ski tips do break and binding bails do fail. Carry a slip-on ski tip, stout cord, and extra binding bails.
- If you have no slip-on ski tip and your ski breaks, pack a mitt with snow and tie it over the end of the broken ski.
- The safe minimum party is three or four persons.
- If one of your party is injured enough so that he cannot ski downhill but can still walk, spiral cord around his skis to prevent them from sliding.
- If one of your party incurs a disabling injury, you should make sure that he is kept warm to prevent hypothermia. Everyone should empty his pack and wrap all available material around the injured person. The material should be kept in place with a waterproof tarp. The injured person should also

be isolated from the snow by lying on his skis
covered with the empty packs.
- For rescue service, ask the telephone operator to
connect you with the nearest local forest ranger.
He has rescue capability.

Travel Over Ice

A fragile mantle of snow can quickly conceal thin ice or
even open water. In picking stream crossings, test the
ice ahead with the point of your ski pole. Ice is almost
always thin where streams enter or leave a lake and
near any spot of open water.

Heavy snows cause ice on lakes to settle, forcing water
up through the cracks that result. This ice slush,
which is seldom visible, may freeze on contact with ski
bottoms. This slush is often local in nature. The first
person through usually has no problem, but the
person following will encounter exposed slush that will
stick to and freeze on his skis. If the track looks dark
ahead, move quickly to the side and make a fresh track.

Clothing

Nordic skiing is very warming exercise because you
use both your arms and your legs. Therefore, it is best
to dress in light, easily ventilated clothing worn in
layers that can easily be adjusted to suit conditions.
A pair of gaiters are recommended to keep the snow
out of your boots and as an aid to keep feet warm. A
windproof parka with a good hood and a thick wool hat
are essential if you are exposed to wind. A scarf to tie
over your face or to warm your neck is a valuable
accessory. In reserve should be a down jacket and

perhaps a down vest. Always carry a spare pair of mitts. Avoid cotton trousers or all-cotton underwear, as these soak up both perspiration and snow-melt and lose their insulating value quickly. Wool, polyester, or acrylic fabrics are preferable.

About Your Automobile

Driving in winter is a large enough subject to be worthy of a whole chapter itself. We have simply noted here a few suggestions that ski tourers on an outing may find particularly useful.

If you drive through heavy snow when the interior of the car is warm, some snow-melt may creep into your door locks and window seals. If you leave your car in this condition on a cold day, you may not be able to get back into it if this water has time to freeze. To protect your locks and windows against freezing, we suggest you keep a can of de-icer fluid in your car and spray this into your door locks and along the window felts before leaving.

Other winter precautions include carrying a snow shovel, chains, sand, and a tow rope. Be sure your antifreeze is at full strength and your battery is in good shape.

If your car is to be parked outdoors on a subzero night, warm it up before going to bed, and while it is warming up shovel a blanket of snow over the hood, around the radiator grille, and around the car's bottom so the entire front end is buried. Snow is a good insulator. Although you will have some light shoveling to do the next morning, the heat thus retained may save you a tow-truck visit.

The Lake Ontario Snowstorms

In addition to the general snowstorms that move across the United States, northwestern New York has an additional snow source all its own: "the lake effect storm."

When strong, cold west or northwest winds sweep over the length of Lakes Erie and Ontario, moisture evaporated from them is carried aloft to form linear snowstorms, each from 100 to 150 miles long but only about 20 miles wide. The intensity of these storms, locally called squalls, has to be experienced to be believed. Snow can fall at the rate of five or six inches an hour, and accumulations can reach two or more

Snow accumulation is substantial where the winds of the lake effect storms have a clean sweep across the Tug Hill Plateau

feet in a single afternoon. As these storms are always accompanied by driving winds, visibility is nil. The driving hazard is extreme. Lake Erie freezes over in the latter part of the winter, while Lake Ontario rarely freezes at all. Therefore Lake Ontario is the principal contributor to these snowstorms.

Modern satellite photography shows that, when conditions are right, six to twelve long, narrow bands of snow clouds form over both these lakes parallel to the wind direction with clear or only partly cloudy conditions between them. When the wind blows from the west, you can drive on the New York Thruway (I-90) across New York unaware that blinding snowstorms are in progress to your north. When the winds are from the northwest or north, however, these storms blow over the major east-west highways from Utica west to Buffalo, so it is not unknown that I-90 is temporarily closed to traffic.

These storms only occur when the forecast calls for a sharp change to colder weather accompanied by strong west to northwest winds. The conditions that cause these storms are easy to forecast, but because their effect is confined to shifting bands perhaps twenty miles wide, it is difficult to pinpoint the exact paths they will follow.

The snowfall from these storms is also sensitive to elevation. Starting from lake elevation at the plain on the eastern shore of Lake Ontario, the ground rises gradually over a distance of about thirty miles to an elevation of almost 2,000 feet at the top of the Tug Hill Plateau. The intensity of snowfall increases accordingly. The elevation then drops steeply into the Black River valley, but rises again to 2,000 to 3,000 feet on the western slopes of the Adirondack Mountains.

These effects are illustrated in the accompanying
snowfall map of New York. The closely spaced lines of
increasing snowfall just east of Lake Ontario are the
result of the snow clouds being pushed up this wedge-
shaped landform. The extraordinary snowfall in a
small zone on top is the result of an additional effect:
the point of convergence of a number of possible storm
tracks from both the west and the northwest. This
zone also corresponds with the highest point of land in
this area. The snow clouds that pass over the Tug Hill
Plateau soon encounter the even higher slopes of the
Adirondack Mountains near Old Forge. Here additional
precipitation is wrung out of the clouds by the higher
elevation.

The lake effect storms are felt over the entire Adirondack area and in the Mohawk River valley as far east as
Albany. The effect diminishes with increasing distance
from Lake Ontario.

If you hear a weather forecast for the region east of
Lake Ontario predicting "snow flurries and snow
squalls likely, one to three inches accumulation
possible, *more snow in the persistent squally areas*,"
you can expect blinding snow and heavy accumulations on I-81 from Syracuse northward in the area
from Parish to Adams Center, and on parallel north-
south roads. You also can anticipate difficult driving
conditions going north from Utica on NY 12 from
Remsen to Lowville or on NY 28 from Alder Creek to
well past Old Forge. Never, never attempt to drive on
the high ground of the Tug Hill Plateau itself in the face
of such a forecast.

Special warnings are needed when crossing the Tug
Hill Plateau on the only available road, NY 177, from
Lowville to Adams Center. It is possible to have good
driving conditions at either end but heavy snowfall

with much blowing and drifting snow on the top.
Most of this road runs through miles of open fields, so
the wind gets a tremendous sweep. The rule is that if
you encounter deteriorating conditions anywhere on
this road, *turn around at once and get out.*

The local highway departments in these areas have
large snow removal budgets, and plenty of equipment.
They usually wait until the worst of these storms is
over and then swing into action. The roads are then
opened in a very short time. These highway crews can
take in stride a snowfall that would cripple other areas
for days.

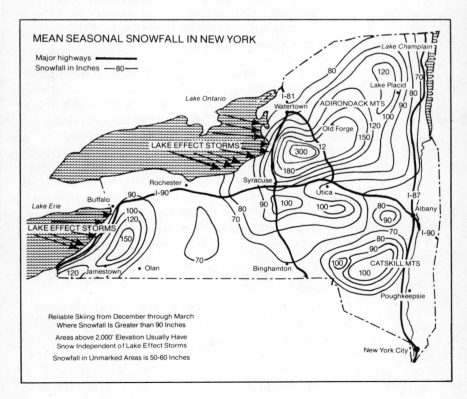

In terms of the tours in this book, Whetstone Gulf and
the Lesser Wilderness State Forest, both off NY 12 and
close to the Snow Ridge ski area at Turin, are on the
eastern edge of the Tug Hill area. Because access to
them is in the Black River valley, the driving is protected from the worst effects of these storms.

Tug Hill State Forest and Jefferson County Forest, near
Barnes Corners on NY 177, are right on top of the Tug
Hill Plateau in highly exposed locations where the
annual snowfall is from twenty to thirty feet. They are
fascinating places to visit but be sure to pick your day
when you go. As a final warning, be prepared. Carry
extra clothing, sleeping bags, and a snow shovel. Also
have a credit card in case you decide to hole up
somewhere unexpectedly.

We don't mean to make the Tug Hill Plateau sound like
a fearsome place. The area offers wonderful skiing, and
a number of ski clubs now active there provide a full
winter program. Some of these organized activities
include such adventuresome trips as a carefully
planned and organized winter crossing of the plateau,
a distance of some twenty miles on skis, and a ski tour
through Inman Gulf, a twelve-mile journey all downhill.
Simply remember that the Tug Hill Plateau is in some
ways like the seashore. People have enjoyable holidays
at the shore, but they don't set out in small boats
during a storm.

*For a continuously updated weather forecast, call:
315-788-2500.*
*Local AM radio stations are WWNY, 790 kHz, Water-
town, and WSYR, 570 kHz, Syracuse.*
*For conditions on the top of the Tug Hill Plateau, call
the Barnes Corners Hotel: 315-688-2934.*
*For conditions at the Whetstone Gulf State Park,
call: 315-376-6630.*

How to Use This Guide

You will notice that certain information has been summarized at the beginning of each of the twenty-five tours. The tour *distance* is always round trip, unless otherwise noted. Round trip may mean around a loop or out and back along the same track. The *map* listings note the name(s) of the appropriate topographical sheet(s) issued by the United States Geological Survey for the area the tour traverses. These maps will be in either the 7½-minute or the 15-minute series and are available at most sporting goods stores or from the USGS itself. (For an index and price list, write: Branch of Distribution, U.S. Geological Survey, 1200 South Eads Street, Arlington, Virginia 22202.) We have also listed other maps that are readily available that we feel will be useful to tourers.

We have also tried at the outset to summarize the terrain you will encounter on each tour and to highlight the special features of each area. These brief descriptions should help you choose tours that match your skiing ability, and we hope they will entice you to read further.

You will also notice that each tour is accompanied by a sketch map. These maps should help you visualize the route we describe and the relative location of particular features we mention. On these maps north is usually at the top. Other standard cartographic symbols are used as follows:

Tour route ■ ■ ■ ■➤   Plowed roads ▬▬▬▬▬
Other trails ••••••••••   Buildings ■
Unplowed roads ═══   Points of interest ✳

Do not rely solely on these sketch maps; you should also carry with you the appropriate USGS sheet(s), especially on wilderness area tours.

1 Boulder Rock

Distance: 5 miles
Map: USGS 15' Kaaterskill
Old carriage road, easy grades; spectacular views
from cliff edge

Boulder Rock is an erratic deposited by a glacier at the edge of a cliff overlooking the Hudson River valley south of Catskill. The ski trail leading to this oddity follows an old carriage road built to serve the grand cliff-top resort hotels that catered to wealthy New Yorkers in the middle nineteenth century. This route is good for beginners, and the views off the escarpment are outstanding.

The starting point for driving directions is the village of Haines Falls on NY 23A, but if your approach is from the floor of the Hudson River valley, you will first have to come through Palenville and the Kaaterskill Clove. The drive up the deep ravine of the Kaaterskill, with ice falls on the left and views of the great cliffs above on the right, is worth the trip by itself.

In Haines Falls, turn to the north at a sign for North Lake, near the Villa Maria resort and the Two Guys From Italy restaurant. Pass Laurel Road and 2.2 miles from NY 23A, turn to the right at Scutt Road, also marked with a Department of Environmental Conservation (DEC) sign to the Kaaterskill Falls. This road goes down a hill, crosses a bridge, and comes to an end in a parking lot. As you cross the bridge you will see the large iron gate that bars motor vehicles from the old carriage roads beyond.

This land along the escarpment was acquired by the
state of New York as the grand old hotels that once
flourished here fell into disrepair. Part of it, near North
Lake, is now given over to a large public campsite, but
the route of this tour is over land largely left unchanged
since the nineteenth century. The area is very popular
in summer with hikers and walkers, so the roads and
paths are marked with color-coded DEC trail disks.
Three of these start out at or very close to the parking
lot.

As you enter the parking lot the blue-marked
Escarpment Trail is to the extreme right. It follows
directly along the line of cliffs and was a favorite with
nineteenth-century artists and lovers. Regretably, only
limited portions are useful to skiers. Sections may be
covered with ice, and downhill stretches make sharp
bends close to the cliff edge. To your left in the parking

Looking south to Indian Head Mountain from Boulder Rock

lot you will notice the iron barrier. A red-marked trail leads from behind it and immediately beyond, a third trail with yellow ski trail markers forks to the left. You might think that you should be following the ski trail markers. Not so. These yellow disks lead only to the public campsite on a dead-level route.

Having sorted this all out, put on your skis and go up the red trail behind the barrier. Stay with the red markers at the first fork; shortly you will come to a second. The way right, marked with yellow disks indicating a horse trail, goes directly for 3/8 mile to the escarpment overlooking the Kaaterskill Clove. The tour to Boulder Rock continues with the red markers on the left-hand fork.

Where the trail curves to the north, or left, you will see the dark green leaves of the mountain laurel contrasted against the snow. This place is lovely in the late spring, for then the entire forest floor is covered with laurel and native pinkster azalea in full flower.

One mile from the start you come to a trail crossing. The way left goes uphill to a clearing where the proud Kaaterskill House once stood. To the right, there is a downhill run to the edge of the escarpment; here it is possible to ski perhaps ¼ mile along the cliff edge. *This downhill side trip is not recommended for beginners.* Straight ahead, the red markers continue to indicate the route to Boulder Rock.

About ¼ mile from the crossing watch for a trail on the right and a sign for Boulder Rock. Here the tour leaves the old carriage road to follow a footpath to the huge rock. Beyond a descent, perhaps 50 feet long, the trail is level. An airplane crashed near here more than ten years ago, and its wreckage is still visible. The trail now

swings to the left and comes out on the edge of the
cliffs. Great blocks of rock have begun to separate from
the mountain, creating narrow crevices in the cliff face.
Boulder Rock is now almost in sight, and the panorama
of the Hudson River valley is below you. The view has
meaning, for in that flat plain and broad river are
written events and trends that shaped the lifestyle of
America today.

In the early history of this country, the Appalachian
mountain chain stood as a formidable barrier to the
passage of commerce from the eastern seaboard to the
west. The Hudson River breaches this range near West
Point, offering a tidewater route inland. Robert Fulton
established steamboat service on the Hudson to
Albany in 1807. The Erie Canal was opened in 1820,
linking the harbor at New York to Lake Erie, and thus
to all the Great Lakes and to the entire midwest. The
canal was followed by the railroad, and the commerce
that built a nation flowed up and down the Hudson in

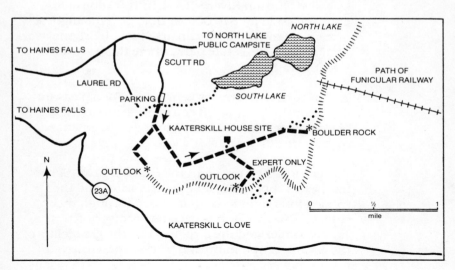

front of where you now stand. The city of New York was raised to its state of grandeur because the resources of a continent flowed past its doors.

Wealthy New Yorkers of the 1850s and 1860s would take the Hudson River steamboat past the Hudson Highlands and Storm King Mountain to a landing and then be driven by stagecoach up the Kaaterskill Clove to their vacation lodgings. Later, the Mountain House, the largest and most prestigious of these hostelries, built a funicular railway right up the face of the escarpment to avoid the long stagecoach drive. If you look to the left you can see the powerline that follows the route of the now-abandoned cable-car railway.

Continue along the escarpment edge until you reach Boulder Rock. Let your eyes follow the Hudson north to the Rip Van Winkle Bridge. Just beyond it on the eastern shore is Olana, the restored hilltop home of Frederick Church, one of the greatest artists of the so-called Hudson River School. In 1859 one of his paintings sold for $10,000, at that time the highest price ever paid an American artist for an original work. That site is now a state park, where there are also ski touring trails.

Your return trip retraces your route. For a pleasant diversion, bear left when you come again to the yellow-blazed horse trail and take it to the escarpment edge that overlooks Kaaterskill Clove.

The grand hotels are gone, the Hudson River School has been supplanted by other art forms, and the tremendous commerce that flowed through the Hudson River valley has been partly diverted by the tractor-trailer and the airplane. But the great cliffs of the escarpment remain and bear silent witness to these changes.

2 Rensselaerville State Forest

Distance: 3 miles
Maps: USGS 7.5' Rensselaerville; USGS 7.5' Durham
Level trail with a few moderate grades; viewpoint

Ski touring is a sport that not only offers you a delightful sense of motion, but also provides the chance to explore and discover for yourself new territory. Most trips in this book are described in meticulous detail. Here the detail only applies to one short route that enables you to find a particularly outstanding view of the northern Catskills. What we really hope to do is to introduce you to a large area where potential for Nordic skiing is so far untapped; this is an area to which you can return again and again and always discover something new.

During the Great Depression, the marginal upland farms of New York State began to go bankrupt and farmers were unable to pay their taxes. Normally local governments will sell such lands for the amount of the unpaid taxes, but during the Depression there was no market. Revenues to local towns and villages dwindled. The state finally began to buy up this marginal farmland for reforestation purposes and found that the sale of forest products was a paying proposition. Over 900,000 acres of such lands were eventually acquired for purposes of watershed protection, the marketing of forest products, wildlife habitat, and public recreation. Rensselaerville State Forest is one such acquisition.

In 1977, an extensive program of timber stand
improvement at Rensselaerville resulted in the
creation of numerous woods roads. Routes were
opened up through growth that was formerly too thick
and brushy to be of much interest to skiers. This great
proliferation of woods roads offers ski touring opportunities at every hand. However, these roads are not
marked or identified, so finding your way is very much
an exercise in backwoods navigation. What is offered is
the fun of exploration.

Before setting out, you should have both USGS maps
listed for this tour, in addition to a copy of the map
shown in this book. The USGS maps depict the area's
hills and valleys, while the accompanying sketch map
gives you the location of new woods roads and trails, as
well as current route designations and road changes.

The view to Windham High Peak in the Catskills

The starting point is the village of Rensselaerville, about thirty-five miles southwest of Albany at the end of NY 85. When NY 85 ends in the village, turn right, or west, onto Albany County #353, which is not shown on conventional road maps. In 2.5 miles look for a sign indicating the Edward P. Cass Youth Camp to the left. An unplowed road leads to the right, or north, opposite. Park along the shoulder of the county road. Just beyond the sign and almost exactly opposite the unplowed road, a woods road departs to the south; this is the start of the trail.

The objective of the route described here is the viewpoint overlooking the Catskills. Within 1/3 mile you will encounter a crossroad. Take the right-hand road, which immediately climbs fairly steeply. To the left as you climb there is a beautiful glade of red and white pines, which allows for skiing in any direction and is fun to explore. The trail will then go down a long easy hill. Just after passing the bottom, you will see a woods road leaving to the left; this logging road comes to a dead-end. The main trail makes a left-hand turn about 1/4 mile farther on. Another 1/3 mile will bring you to a Department of Environmental Conservation (DEC) truck trail, usually unplowed, that passes near the viewpoint.

Follow it to the top of the first rise, where you will find openings on both sides of the road. Leaving the truck trail, move into the area to the south, or left. It is dotted with white pines and scrub growth. You have to climb very slightly to get out of the truck trail, whereupon the view of Windham High Peak and other mountains of the northern Catskills will begin to appear. The best outlook is 1/4 mile ahead.

This viewpoint is the end of the official tour. If you lack outdoor navigation skills, you might wish to retrace your steps to the car, a distance of 1½ miles. But if you are the adventuresome type and wish to add to your sense of exploration, here are some possibilities.

The trail map in this book shows the approximate location of a former homestead with a cellar hole and a stone well that still has water in it, lying generally west of where you stand and near Scutt Road. See if you can discover them.

Going generally west from the viewpoint and staying on the brow of the hill, you will be in the open. A strip of hardwoods lies ahead, enclosing an old road that leads to Scutt Road. In our explorations, we always seem to run on this old road, but even if you don't find it, the woods have been thinned enough so skiing is pleasant through them.

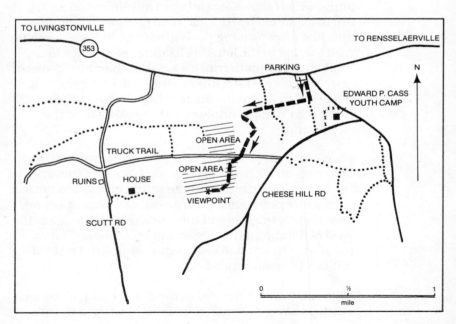

There is also good glade skiing through well-thinned plantation pines to the north of the DEC truck trail. The opportunities here are so numerous that it will take you many trips before you have exhausted them all.

This area has a long snow season, so there is often one or two feet of snow here when there is none in Albany. We recall coming here in the late spring for a winter picnic with steak, dark bread, and red wine, and rolling up our shirt sleeves to luxuriate in the drenching sunshine. We then skied through the cool shade of the deep pine glades, which offered such a contrast to the brilliance of the sunlit open areas that it took a while for our eyes to adjust to the dark.

In going or coming through the village of Rensselaerville, you will be impressed by the stately white-painted buildings, more typical of New England villages than of New York. Rensselaerville, named for the old Dutch patroon, Van Rensselaer, was the former mercantile capital of this area. The village radiates good taste and affluence. The principal buildings date from 1809 to 1830, all designed by the architect Ephraim Ross. They are sculptures in white pine. The early maps of Albany County show two principal towns, the port of Albany and the city of Rensselaerville. The brook that rushes through the village was an important source of power for the early Huyck felt mill upstream from the bridge and for a grist mill now being restored just downstream of the bridge. The Huyck Felt Company, which started here, is an important industry in the region, but is now located just across the river from Albany.

3 Partridge Run

Distance: 4 miles
Map: USGS 7.5' Rensselaerville
Wide trails with a few steep grades; long snow season

This tour runs through a wildlife management area on a high plateau that lies about thirty miles southwest of Albany. The elevation, almost 2,000 feet, gives it a long snow season, and driving time to it from the center of the Capital District is about forty minutes. The route described here is over unplowed town roads and very wide hunter access trails, so is suitable for skiers of all abilities. Because of its good snow cover, proximity to Albany, and extensive trail system, Partridge Run has become one of the more popular cross-country skiing locations in this area.

This attractiveness is enhanced by an administrative policy that divides the area into motorized and nonmotorized zones, thus separating snowmobilers and ski tourers. However, this policy does not apply to the unplowed town roads, which the state does not regulate and thus are open to all public use.

This is the only trip in the book that utilizes a wildlife management area. The nation's hunters were the first to appreciate that their sport depended upon maintaining viable habitats for the various types of game species. They were successful in obtaining Federal legislation to tax ammunition to create a land acquisition fund that would help meet that goal. Partridge Run was acquired with the sportsmen's dollars, and it is set aside primarily for public hunting and fishing. The land was once farmed, so you will see old stone walls, cellar holes, the ruins of a church, and an old burying ground.

This land has a turbulent history. Originally it was part of Rensselaerswyck, the large manor (it covered an area 24 miles wide by 48 miles long) established in 1630 by the Dutch patroon, Killian Van Rensselaer. In the 1600s wealthy Dutchmen, titled patroons, could acquire huge tracts of lands, called wycks, in the American Dutch colonies. The patroons were not only landholders; they were also the sole administrators of justice in their holdings, and they possessed permanent seats in legislative bodies and could thus perpetuate their power. Dutch settlers were enticed to work on these holdings by promises of ten years' freedom from rents. After this time rents were imposed. However, under pain of arbitrary punishment, they could not leave the land, nor seek other employment, nor build any other structure on the land without the permission of the patroon. In 1664 when the English took over the Dutch colonies, the patroon system was recognized *in toto* by the British Crown. Such was the economic and political power of the patroons that this system of serfdom straight out of the Middle Ages actually survived the American Revolution.

Stephen Van Rensselaer, known as "the good," came into this estate just after the Revolution. He treated his tenants generously and forgave payments of much of the rents. His son Stephen Jr. kept careful account of all omitted payments, and on the death of his father in 1839 demanded the unpaid rents under threat of immediate eviction. This would have resulted in most of the farmers in his domain being dispossessed, and an anti-rent movement grew to the point of armed rebellion. The sheriff's posses from Albany who attempted to serve eviction notices often fled these hills for their lives.

The Van Rensselaers eventually gave up their attempts to collect these rents and sold their interests for fifty cents on the dollar to an unscrupulous speculator named Colonel Church. He formed a corrupt alliance with the sheriff and a judge, and with the law and the courts behind him sought to gain possession of all those farms from Altamont to Knox to Berne to Rensselaerville that owed rents. You will pass through or near these towns on your way to Partridge Run. Church's agents were tarred and feathered; sheriff's deputies were shot from ambush, and the militia made four separate invasions of this territory to suppress the anti-rent movement. These disturbances did not cease until after the Civil War.

Lunching at the edge of the pine plantation

Agriculture on the highest parts of this territory was only profitable during the early and middle nineteenth century. The colder climate, overgrazing of sheep, and the depletion and erosion of soil made farming marginal here by the turn of this century. It completely collapsed during the Depression. Abandoned agricultural lands were sold to the State during this period for perhaps a dollar an acre. This is how Partridge Run came into public ownership.

As you will be driving on the back roads in Albany County not shown on state road maps, keep the accompanying sketch map handy. The starting point is the hamlet of Berne at the intersection of NY 443 and NY 156. Leave town going west on NY 443, and just beyond the Berne Central School, bear left at a Y fork off NY 443. In less than a mile you will intersect Switz Kill Road (Albany Co. #1). Turn left here, and then right at the next turn, Sickle Hill Road (Albany Co. #13). It goes across some flats and then starts to climb an extremely steep hill, going around a hairpin bend and making reverse turns. Just beyond the top there is a sharp turn to the left. Within a mile you will see a ruined church (circa 1850) on your right. Stop just beyond it by an unplowed road to the right marked as Beaver Road; the snowplow frequently makes a parking area at the entrance. Do not block the private driveway that is perhaps fifty feet in from the main road on the left.

The Partridge Run area has a complicated set of trails branching off the old farm roads that run through it. None of the intersections have signs, and consequently you should carry with you a copy of the map in this guide; the USGS sheet shows the roads but none of the new ski trails. To minimize confusion, each trail junction on your map has been labeled to correspond with the text. There are no such marks on the ground.

The tour will take you counter-clockwise around a loop, so the first turn will be to the right, and thereafter every turn will be to the left. We have also mentioned two side trips of less than ¼ mile each, one to a viewpoint and the other to an old cemetery.

Start off down Beaver Road, and in 1/3 mile turn to the right on a side trail (A). Soon you enter an open area and turn left at (B). The route leads over a dam for a fishing pond to your right, climbs slightly, and enters woods. A downgrade follows that terminates in a right-hand turn in some big white pines. The trail now winds its way through some tall hemlock and pine

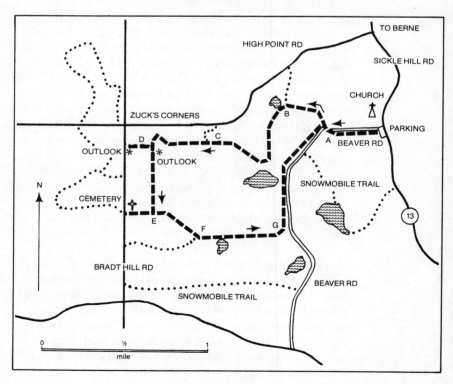

plantations to junction (C). Here you go straight and shortly swing to the right as the trail climbs a steep slope. It reverses direction at the top, where there is a fine view over the ground you have just covered. Behind you on the brow of the hill is a heavy stand of white pines. You are now at or very close to junction (D). Take a side trip by going through the pines to an open field, where the view really opens up to the west toward the Schoharie Valley, and then return to junction (D).

The route now goes along the top of the slope and enters another pine plantation where you will meet with junction (E). To visit the cemetery bear right, skiing down to the Bradt Hill Road. To your right you will see the old tombstones sticking up through the snow. Some of the burial markers date to the 1840s. Then retrace your route to junction (E). Coming back from the cemetery you will go straight and enter a succession of downgrades, which become steeper toward the bottom. You will pass junction (F) on the way down. After crossing a dam at the end of another small pond, you have a short climb followed by another downhill run through a field. You finally come out at junction (G) on Beaver Road. Turn left, skiing down a very satisfactory hill, and return to your start.

When you have completed this tour, you will have become more familiar with the area. The map shows possibilities for more extensive trips. This area is excellent for late season skiing when the snow may all be gone in the Capital District, and indeed for most of the automobile trip out. In late March and early April the snow usually holds above 1,500 feet in elevation. We have had many an enjoyable trip here well into April.

4 Featherstonhaugh State Forest

Distance: 3½ miles
Maps: USGS 7.5' Rotterdam; USGS 7.5' Duanesburg
Flat and easy grades; beaver colony

Beavers are usually associated with the big north woods, but it happens that there is at least one active beaver colony in the Capital District. It is found about nine miles west of Schenectady in a state forest called Featherstonhaugh.

That unusual name comes by way of Duane Featherstonhaugh, a settler who about 1800 acquired a 50,000-acre landholding that stretched all the way from Duanesburg west to Schoharie Creek. He introduced novel farming methods to the area, owned sheep numbering in the thousands, and gave his name to Duane Lake, Featherstonhaugh Lake, and the town of Duanesburg.

In 1955 the state of New York floated a bond issue to acquire lands for the multiple uses of forestry, watershed protection, wildlife habitat, and public outdoor recreation. The tract of land south of Featherstonhaugh Lake was purchased through this program and was named for the lake it borders.

Featherstonhaugh's beaver pond is scarcely ¼ mile from the principal road that traverses the forest. For such a short distance it is hardly worthwhile putting your skis in the car, but fortunately there are also about 2¼ miles of ski touring trails in the same state forest. By combining a trip to the pond with a whirl around the trails, the tour will be about 3½ miles long, and you will have a novel objective and a more interesting place to lunch.

To reach Featherstonhaugh, take NY 159 west from Schenectady toward Mariaville. Six miles after you go under I-90 and 1.5 miles from Weast Road turn left on Lake Road. Follow this road around Featherstonhaugh Lake, and at the top of a rise note a signboard on the right indicating you are entering the state forest. In another .3 mile Tidball Road enters from the left; about 300 feet beyond this intersection look on the left for a brown sign with yellow letters reading "Ski Touring Trail." Park here alongside the road. Note that this road traversing the forest enters on the east as Lake Road and emerges on the west as Highland Park Road. This curious metamorphosis occurs at a junction with an

Investigating the snow-covered beavers' house

unplowed, unmarked dirt lane the locals call Spook Road, which leads to the beaver pond.

The first few hundred feet of trail are actually an access route to an interior loop; a second access leads from Highland Park Road almost diagonally across the loop from where you are standing. The trail continues on the western side of Highland Park Road in the form of a figure-eight. This tour takes you out one side of the loop, around the figure-eight, and back on the other half of the first loop, where you make the short detour to the beaver pond.

Starting at the Lake Road entrance, ski down the access road and bear left at the first trail junction. In about 1 mile the trail forks again. Highland Park Road is straight ahead, while the way to your right will be your return.

Before starting the figure-eight, ski uphill, to your left, on Highland Park Road. When you reach the top of the rise you will have a fine view of the Catskills and the Normanskill. Then return nearly to the point where you emerged from the woods and pick up the figure-eight on your left.

When you have completed that circuit, return to the trail junction at the Highland Park Road end of the first loop, and ski the fork you ignored on the way out. This trail does not bring you directly to Spook Road, the route to the beaver pond, only close to it. Watch carefully for the point where the trail makes an obvious bend to the right, changing direction from north to east. You are now close enough to Lake Road that if a car goes past, you will see it. About 100 feet farther, the ski trail crosses the small creek that flows north to the beaver pond.

Between the corner and the stream ski through the woods to the road and then turn left. The twin signs that mark the entrance to Spook Road will be in view. Spook Road bends to the left as it skirts the base of a small wooded hill. The woods on the left shortly give way to field. At this point a glance to your right will show the tall dead trees typical of beaver flooding. Make your way through the scrub directly out on the beaver pond.

When we were there, there was a large beaver house a little past the middle of the pond. The beaver house has

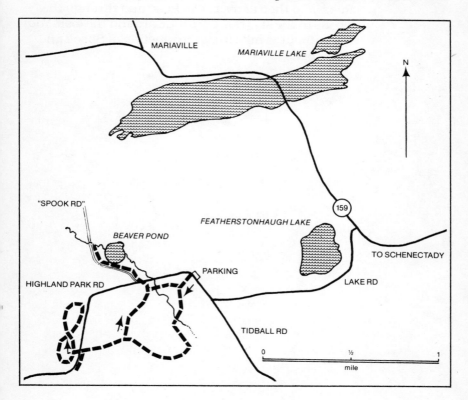

a floor above water level and an underwater entrance. In winter, beavers must swim out under the ice to some point of open water before they can emerge. They often don't have to come out at all, for beavers store their winter food supply underwater and can simply swim to their larder and back again.

The northern fringe of this pond is sheltered from the wind by heavy evergreen growth. The sun beats in on this protected area, making it an excellent lunch spot.

To return to your car, retrace your tracks on Spook Road, and then across Lake Road and through the woods to the ski trail. Continue around the loop. Your car is about ½ mile from the junction of Spook and Lake roads.

5 Plotterkill Preserve

Distance: 4 miles
Maps: USGS 7.5' Rotterdam Junction; county map
Route along the rim of a steep-sided ravine, three
significant hills; overlooks to the Mohawk Valley and
Schenectady

Imagine a scene 9,000 years ago, at the end of the most recent Ice Age. Masses of ice some two miles high were melting rapidly, releasing surging torrents of water with energy enough to move and reshape vast amounts of earth and rock. The effects of the retreating glacier on the local landscape are seen everywhere in Schenectady County, but in few places are they as dramatic as in the narrow box canyon just west of Schenectady known as the Plotterkill. Here a retreating waterfall created the steep-sided gorge when its plummeting water undercut the resistant caprock to maintain a vertical drop. The gorge is now some two miles long and has at its upper end three waterfalls, one seventy feet high.

Schenectady County has acquired a strip of land on both sides of the Plotterkill for public use and maintains a trail along the ravine's rim, which you follow on this tour. A trail map for the Plotterkill Preserve is available from the Schenectady County Planning Department, 630 State Street, Schenectady, NY 12305. Access to the trail is confined to two short stretches of county property that front on public roads. To reach the section on Coplon Road where you find the trailhead, drive west on NY 159 from Schenectady toward Mariaville. Coplon Road is on the right (north) side of the road, 2.8 miles beyond the I-90 overpass. Follow Coplon Road for .7 mile to a turn-around where

the road enters private lands. Reverse your direction
and park alongside the road near the first hedgerow,
about 500 feet back down the road. The trail, marked
with orange fluorescent tape, starts by a sign for
Plotterkill Preserve at the corner of the hedgerow.
Please bear in mind that the field beyond is privately
owned, as is a natural gas pipeline right-of-way, which
looks like an access, just before the hedgerow. (The
pipeline right-of-way should also be avoided because it
goes over the brow of a hill and then dives into the
ravine at a very steep angle.)

From the trailhead you have a panorama of the hills
that rise above the Mohawk Valley, which lies to your
right. The trail enters the grove of white pines almost
directly below you, but you might wish to follow a
zigzagging course across the field to ease the grade.
About 500 feet into the woods, you cross the pipeline
right-of-way and continue through a hemlock forest
parallel to the ravine.

After passing under an electric transmission line and
climbing diagonally up a steep sidehill, you must
descend a twisting path to get around a gully that
plunges into the main ravine in a series of vertical
drops. The trail is laid out so as to stay well back from
these cliffs. Once past the gully, the trail skirts the
ravine's rim, offering a number of glimpses through
the trees of the gorge below, and then comes out in an
open field.

Up to this point, the boundary between private and
county lands has been roughly the edge of the woods.
This field, however, is county land. Ahead of you note
the tower of another electric transmission line. Near it
is one of the best overlooks on the tour; the view from
here is northwest, up the Mohawk Valley.

Your destination, a second overlook with views east of
the city of Schenectady, is about ½ mile from the tower.
To reach it, proceed generally parallel to the sides of the
ravine to the woods on the field's northeastern end.
There you will see a trail marked with red flagging tape
entering the woods. It turns to the right and continues
through open oaks and maples generally parallel to the
transmission line.

While the actual overlook is under this transmission
line, the snow in the clear corridor is exposed to wind
and is apt to be crusty, thus affording poorer skiing
than the woods route, which brings you out on the
transmission line about ¼ mile from the overlook. You
are now over the brow of a hill where the snow should
be good, and the view starts to open up. The best view
is where a transmission line comes in from the right;

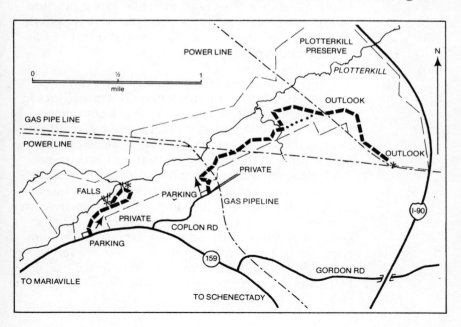

that corridor looks like it would offer a short cut back
to your car. Alas, no! Private property intervenes.

From the overlook, you can see the old Scotia naval
depot on the left, then the village of Scotia and the
Great Western Gateway Bridge; St. John's Church and
Ellis Hospital are prominent landmarks. In the middle
distance is the Schenectady Works of the General
Electric Co. When you are ready to return, head out the
way you came in.

Before leaving Plotterkill Preserve, you may wish to
visit the waterfalls at the end of the gorge. The section
between the pipeline right-of-way and the waterfalls is
so steep as to make an approach by any means from
this direction dangerous. Instead, take your car back
out to NY 159 and proceed west an additional .5 mile,
or ten telephone poles. Look for a plantation of white
pines by the roadside. The second public access to the
Plotterkill is a jeep road blocked by a chain barrier at
the uphill end of the pine plantation.

The trip to the upper falls takes about five minutes.
Take the first left-hand turn where the trail divides to
the upper falls; then follow a trail that leads downstream to the lower falls. To return, you can continue
around the loop or retrace your steps. Because so many
people come to view the ice formations that encase
these falls, the trail may be badly pocked with footprints; if you want to be assured of a good ski track
here, try this side trip just after a snowstorm. In winter
it is best not to attempt to descend into the gorge or
even get too close to the edge—or to cross the stream—
because the banks near the watercourse are very steep
with shale cliffs and the ice may not be as solid as it
looks. Never mind, the view from the top of the gorge is
well worth the trip.

6 Saratoga Battlefield

Distance: 6 miles
Map: available at visitor center
Essentially flat terrain, one moderate hill; historic site

Thirty miles north of Albany the Saratoga Battlefield, officially known as the Saratoga National Historical Park, offers some eleven miles of full-width unplowed roads, many interconnecting informal paths, ski touring trails, extensive fields and meadows, and deep pine and hardwood forests. The deer come out of the forests in winter and graze openly. The skiing here is outstanding.

This land was set aside as a national monument to the Battle of Saratoga, the turning point of the American Revolution. The tour described here makes use of both the marked ski trail laid out by the National Park Service and an unplowed road to the American River fortifications overlooking the Hudson River. This latter area is of interest not only because it is a scenic out-look but because from here your eyes can appreciate at once the canny strategy of the Americans and how they utilized land features to force the battle to take place under circumstances to their advantage.

The Saratoga National Historic Park is shown on most road maps, and major nearby highways have signs directing visitors to the main entrance and parking area. The most useful approach for most will be via the Adirondack Northway (I-87). Take I-87 to Exit 21 and go east, through the village of Malta. One mile east of

I-87, at a Y intersection, turn left on Saratoga County #108. Turn right on NY 9P at the shore of Saratoga Lake. Just beyond the end of the lake a sign directs you to the right toward the park; continue to follow the signs from here.

A walkway leads from the parking lot to the Visitor Center (phone: 518-664-9821), where an information desk has maps and brochures. There are exhibits, a museum, and a theater for presentations on the battle and on eighteenth-century life. The National Park Service discourages use of the Visitor Center as a lunchroom, so plan to have your snacks on the trail or in the car.

This tour starts at the Visitor Center and continues south along a ridge with extensive overlooks of the fields below and views of the mountains of Vermont in the background. The most prominent peak is Willard Mountain, directly across the Hudson. It was here the Americans placed a signal team with spyglasses and naval signal flags to report on British movements.

The trail will swing to the left, and you will go zipping and bumping down the tour's only really significant hill and come flying out in a field. You will not notice that the return route joins the trail you are now on at the bottom because you go by so fast! This descent is followed by a small climb and a second downgrade, beyond which the route is almost flat.

While skiing across the field dotted with big white pines, you will notice to your left a ring of stakes and an assemblage of cannon. The map shows that this was the site of a palisaded British redoubt commanded by Lieutenant-Colonel Von Breymann. Just behind it, in the woods and surrounded by an iron fence, is a curious memorial to Benedict Arnold, showing only his memorialized wounded leg.

The trail drops down onto an unplowed park road, and shortly the log cabin of Freeman's Farm will come into view. This point can be confusing, for the marked ski trail goes straight ahead, but as everyone wants to see the cabin the ski tracks go in that direction. After checking out the cabin yourself, return to the marked trail. Continuing south, you will pass the site of a second powerful British field fortification, this one commanded by the Earl of Balcarres.

After entering the woods, the trail forks. Take the left-hand route, which drops into a ravine. A short distance beyond, the trail forks again; again bear left, leaving the marked route. In 1¼ miles you will come to the American River fortifications.

The Freeman's Farm log cabin with Willard Mountain in the background

Here you will stand overlooking the floodplain of the
Hudson River, squeezed at this point between high
bluffs. Below you, the hillside bristles with pointed
stakes and timber obstructions. Behind these defenses
American cannon are emplaced, trained on the valley
below.

In the summer of 1777 the British General Burgoyne
marched south from Canada toward Albany, and in the
trackless American wilderness of that period the only
feasible route in this area was a road along the Hudson
River valley bottom. Part of this original route is visible
today close to the river. The fortifications where you
stand blocked his advance. The steep banks of the
Hudson just to the north are cut with deep ravines,
which on the morning of the battle on that early
autumn day were filled with dense fog. Burgoyne had
no choice but to work his way inland so as to avoid
these obstacles.

The British distrusted fighting from behind trees
Indian-style. Their military doctrine called for set-piece
engagements in open areas where their superior
discipline and organization might prevail. The only
open areas in the wilderness were the farms near
Freeman's cabin, which you passed, and the Barber
wheatfield, which you will see on your return. This is
how the land influenced military strategy.

When you return to the Visitor Center you can see a
theater presentation on how the battle was won. You
will learn that the first engagement took place near the
Freeman's Farm cabin, when Colonel Daniel Morgan
rallied his Pennsylvania riflemen by imitating the call
of the wild turkey. You will also learn of Benedict
Arnold's wild charge through the crossfire of both
armies, leading his men over the rear of the Breymann

redoubt, an action that capped the final victory. Your appreciation of the exhibits and the historical material in the center will be sharpened by having gone over the ground with your own two feet.

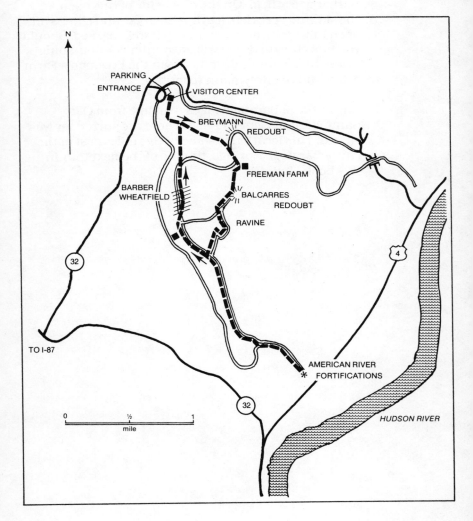

Return the way you came until you pick up the ski trail markers again. Now take the left-hand fork in order to continue the loop. The trail, which is following an unplowed park road, will leave the woods and enter the Barber wheatfield. On the other side of this open area, the ski trail veers left, leaving the road, and climbs an open hillside. This junction is not well marked. Should you miss the turn, you will encounter your outgoing tracks at a point midway between the Freeman's Farm cabin and the Breymann redoubt.

The Battle of Saratoga takes its name from Old Saratoga, now Schuylerville, where the surrender was signed. This location is some twelve miles east of the city of Saratoga Springs, the site of the next tour in this book (Tour 7).

7 Saratoga Spa

Distance: 5½ miles
Map: available at X-C center
Groomed trails, easy terrain; bubbling mineral
springs, health spa

It was the waters that first brought people to Saratoga Springs. The Iroquois Indians were long aware of a valley from whose sides flowed some 122 bubbling springs that had a tingling salty taste and that seemed to benefit the health. In 1776 the famous Indian diplomat, Sir William Johnson, was stricken with ill health. He was beloved by the Indians, who carried him to these springs. He was the first white man known to have benefited from these waters, and their fame has been spreading ever since.

Today, these same waters flow forth within a magnificent state park with a full winter program. The health spa tradition is maintained in the Roosevelt Baths, which offer mineral water baths, Turkish baths, massages, and both dry and moist heat rooms.

More important to our purposes is the existence of miles of groomed ski trails, and an official 5 km NASTAR race course where cross-country ski races are held weekly. The Saratoga Mountain Ski Touring Center in the center of the park offers rentals, instruction, and a full line of ski equipment and accessories, and the area around the Performing Arts Center is illuminated after dark for nighttime skiing.

Here you can put on your skis, take your cup, and ski from spring to spring sampling the waters. Or you can enjoy a winter picnic at one of the park's numerous picnic tables. For apres-ski, luxuriate in the baths, the massages, and the heat rooms of the Roosevelt Baths, and then take in historic downtown Saratoga Springs, a resort city famous since 1850. All of this is within an hour's drive of the Capital District.

The park is located at the southern end of the city of Saratoga Springs, west of US 9 and east of NY 50. The turnoffs into the park from both these major highways are well marked. Once inside the park, follow the signs to the Saratoga Mountain Ski Touring Center.

Geyser Creek, containing the mineral springs, flows through the park from north to south. It has a flat-floored valley wide enough for an all-season auto road and picnic and recreation areas. Woods roads allow ski

Start of the Citizen Race at the Saratoga Mountain Ski Touring Center

access to the valley from the relatively flat areas above. The eastern bank contains a beautiful deep ravine called the Ferndell, which is marked as a one-way climbing trail because the grade at its upper end is so steep. A park road called the North-South Road runs directly past the point of emergence from the Ferndell and leads north to the parking area and the complex of park buildings that includes the ski touring center. An eighteen-hole golf course lies to the east. The park is thus divided into three zones: the golf course, the area containing the Ferndell, and the area on the far, or west, side of the Geyser Creek valley. The objective is to describe a route that will best feature all three areas.

Start your tour from behind the ski center on the marked trail around the golf course. As you are about to complete the loop and are heading to the center going north, parallel to North-South Road, hop across the road into the deep woods of the Ferndell area. The trail that runs close to the road will shortly turn sharply left and go past the Roosevelt Baths. Just beyond the bath building depart left on a wider woods road. This is the best descent into the Geyser Creek valley. You will come scooting out at the bottom next to the automobile road. When you have stopped, reverse your direction and parallel the road toward the bridge crossing Geyser Creek.

As you approach the bridge, look upstream, where a geyser spurts water ten to fifteen feet into the air. If you have come to drink of the waters, there are three mineral springs close to where you now stand.

To continue the trip, cross the bridge and climb a woods road to the left. It will fork at the top of the hill. Bear right and continue on a trail loop about 1½ miles long that leads past the Peerless Pool summer

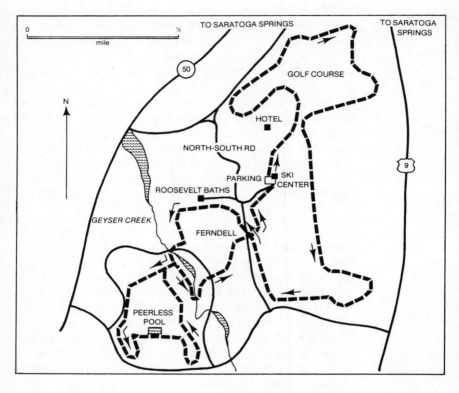

swimming area. Completing the loop, ski back down
into the Geyser Creek valley the way you came out.

We suggest that you return to the ski center via the
Ferndell. Turn to your right, and ski about 700 feet
through a picnic area to a footbridge across Geyser
Creek and continue to the auto road, now almost in
sight. The Ferndell mineral spring is almost directly
across this road, and just beyond is the entrance to the
ravine. You will emerge at the top of the ravine looking
across North-South Road at the golf course. The
parking area is less than ¼ mile to the left.

8 Northville-Placid Trail to Rock Lake

Distance: 9 miles
Map: USGS 15' Lake Pleasant
Wilderness tour; easy grades but narrow trail,
intermediate difficulty

The Northville-Placid Trail was one of the first of the summer hiking trails to be discovered by cross-country skiers. This section is relatively close to the Capital District and is used frequently, so there is a very good chance that others will have broken track for you, making the route all the more attractive. While this southernmost stretch of the trail runs to Piseco, a distance of some twenty-five miles, this tour will only take you as far as Rock Lake and then add a short side trip through a frozen Adirondack vly, or wetland.

The starting point of this part of the Northville-Placid Trail is hardly a mile from the Lapland Lake Ski Touring Center, so the opportunity exists to ski one day at a commercial center and then try some wilderness skiing the next. Accommodations are available at the ski touring center (address: RD 2, Northville, NY 12134; phone: 518-863-4974).

Driving directions are given from the intersection of NY 30 and the road leading to the village of Northville. While this is not a numbered route, the intersection is prominently marked. This intersection is very nearly one hour's driving time from the Albany-Troy-Schenectady area. Continue north on NY 30 for 3.3 miles, and then turn left (west) onto a side road to Benson. Up to this point, NY 30 has been following the Sacandaga River, whose elevation is about 800 feet.

The trailhead elevation is close to 1,500 feet, so there
is some climbing ahead. A good deal of this is accom-
plished in a long hill just after leaving NY 30. If the
snow was marginal coming north on NY 30, you should
see an improvement in the snow cover now. You will
pass a side road on the right to Lapland Lake Ski
Touring Center 5.2 miles from NY 30. At 5.8 miles you
will cross an iron bridge; at the Y-intersection just
beyond, a large hanging signboard directs you right
(north) to the Northville-Placid Trail. Drive .8 mile and
turn left where a sign indicates the route to Rock Lake
and to Silver Lake. The parking lot is .5 mile ahead, on
the right.

Crossing the bridge over the West Branch of Stony Creek

Put on your skis and continue past the parking area;
the road forks just beyond it. The trail goes right,
downhill, following the blue Department of Environmental Conservation (DEC) disks, while the left-hand
fork is a private driveway.

Your skis will have barely stopped sliding from this
downhill ride when you will be in a clearing by an old
hunting camp, the headquarters of the United Rod and
Gun Club. This land is most aggressively posted
against any form of trespass, but be reassured for
there is an easement across this property for public
access. Shortly the trail will climb a fairly long hill that
will afford a real ride on the way back, go over a rise of
ground, and then descend, coming out in the open.
Directly ahead is the wide and fast-flowing West
Branch of Stony Creek, which you reach 1/3 mile from
your start.

The trail now takes a sharp left and follows the creek
another 1/3 mile to a footbridge. There is an attractive
set of falls here that will be all sheathed in ice with the
sound of water gurgling underneath.

You now climb steadily and gradually for the next mile
to the crossing of Goldmine Creek. Iron pyrite, or fool's
gold, was discovered here in the early days. This
section of trail is gullied in summer and thus collects
the meltwater from thaws, so there may be less snow
cover here. This part of the trail may also offer
technical skiing problems. You then cross Goldmine
Creek, an insignificant watercourse, and come to a
long climb that lasts almost ½ mile and will take you
up to 1,900 feet.

This is followed by an easy descent, then another
climb. In 3¾ miles the trail forks; the way left goes to

Rock Lake while the Northville-Placid Trail continues to the right. It is only about ¼ mile down to Rock Lake, so you can almost see it from the main trail. The eastern end of the lake is all in hardwoods, but there is a fine stand of spruce and hemlock at the western end that gives better protection from the wind.

Rock Lake drains to the west through a low marshy outlet. In our trips to this area, we often follow the outlet for about ½ mile to the point where it joins another marsh coming in from the right, or north. By skiing up this second marsh, we enter the woods at the northern end only some 1,000 feet from the Northville-Placid Trail, which is dead ahead. We then take a right-hand or easterly turn, and in about 1 mile pick up our morning's tracks where we diverted to go to Rock Lake.

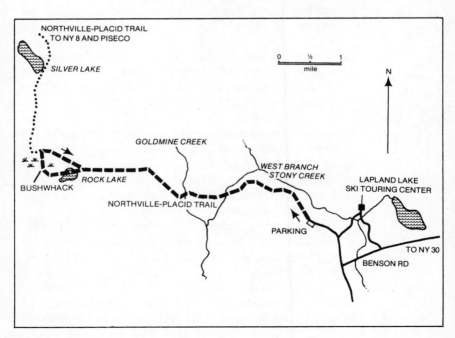

Do not confuse right from left here, for if you turn left
(west), you will be heading into the Silver Lake
Wilderness Area, and you will cover twenty miles before
you will get out of it. You will find that the return trip
offers long and continuous downhill rides, which are
very enjoyable.

There is a general caution that applies to this and
other trails in the Adirondack wilderness; if you are
skiing early in the season when the snow is sparser
than normal, many of the small drainages you cross
and usually don't notice may not be fully frozen over or
have established snow bridges. Every time you come to
one of these you will have to brake—hard if you're
going downhill—and then pick your way across.

9 Pharaoh Lake

Distance: 10 miles
Maps: USGS 15' Paradox Lake; USGS 15' Bolton
Landing
Generally level grade; mountain-rimmed lake

This is a pleasant trip on an old road to an attractive body of water, with an option to return partway along the outlet of Pharaoh Lake through a meadow open enough to offer good views. At the time of our visit, this meadow had an unusually large number of animal tracks: deer, fox, and otter. At one point we saw signs that a fox had climbed on top of a beaver house and had attempted to make a hole in the roof. We could also see where Mr. Beaver had attempted to repair the damage.

The distance from your start to the foot of Pharaoh Lake is almost exactly 4 miles. The point where the lake opens up to afford good views is about 1 mile further, making this a 10-mile round trip. Because the stream crossings are bridged this tour can be taken late in the season.

Take I-87 to Exit 24 (Chestertown and Brant Lake) and take NY 8 to the right, leading to Brant Lake. Follow the shoreline of Brant Lake. At the upper end turn left on Palisades Road, which will take you around the upper end of the lake. The road will veer to the left again and .2 mile beyond this turn, or 1.2 miles from NY 8, you will reach the entrance to Pharaoh Lake Road where you park your vehicle. This unplowed dirt road departs to the right, or north, in a notch between Park Mountain and No. 8 Mountain.

Stopping by Pharaoh Lake Brook

The first part of the tour will be in mixed hardwoods
along an almost level road. There are three summer
camps along this road, the last of which you pass just
before you reach the boundary of the Pharaoh Lake
Wilderness Area, 4/10 mile from the start.

At 1½ miles the notch opens up into the Mill Brook
valley. This is the summer parking area. A marsh lies
ahead so you have your first view of Pharaoh Mountain
with the fire tower here. There is a pleasant vista in
both directions up and down Mill Brook with No. 6 Hill,
the Dam Hill, and No. 8 Hill all visible. A glance at the
USGS map will get you well oriented with respect to
these landmarks.

The barrier that closes the road to motor vehicles is
just ahead of the summer parking lot. Beyond it, the
trail enters plantation pines set some forty years ago
during the Great Depression by the Civilian Conservation Corps. The trail now begins a slow climb that will
amount to some 200 vertical feet. In 2½ miles you will
come to a knoll close to where the trail will cross
Pharaoh Lake Brook on a bridge. This is a scenic spot
and is also quite sheltered, so if you don't want to wait
until you get to the lake for lunch, it is a good place to
take a snack.

From this point on, Pharaoh Lake Brook will
accompany you on your left, or west, side. The brook
actually flows through a marsh or wetland area, and
this is the spot where we saw all the signs of wildlife.
Past the open marsh, at 3 1/3 miles, the brook comes
closer to the trail and is usually open water. You are
now getting close to the narrow outlet end of Pharaoh
Lake, which comes into view at 4 miles.

There is a fish barrier dam at the foot of the lake. A
horse trail, marked with horseshoe markers, and the

summer hiking trail to Pharaoh Mountain both come
in from the left and converge at the dam. As they go
over some higgledy-piggledy ground, they are not
recommended for exploration on skis.

Skiing up the lake is a real pleasure because the view
continually widens as the lake opens up. The first
outlook is to the cliffs on Thunderbolt Mountain and
Grizzle Ocean Mountain to the right. Treadway
Mountain is seen almost dead ahead. As you really
come out into the main part of the lake the big
shoulder of Pharaoh Mountain comes into view to the
the left.

Just north of Pharaoh Lake there's a pond that also
bears the name Grizzle Ocean. In the nineteenth

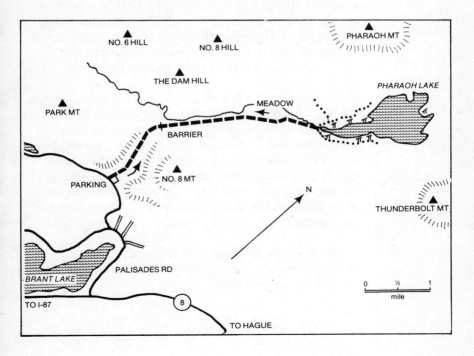

century a trapper named Grizzle built a cabin at this site and was quite territorial about it, so the local legend grew that this was his ocean. Grizzle Ocean Mountain takes its name from the small lake that lies beneath it.

There is some fascinating ski touring to be had in the country to the north, but that area is for experts only. Geologically speaking, the topography is influenced by block faulting, so the terrain is abrupt with many cliffs and ledges. Slopes that may appear to be skiable based on inspection of contour line density on the map in reality are likely to have locally steep spots.

There are seven lean-tos near the southern end of the lake: three on the western shore and four on the eastern side. An eighth lean-to is found on a point of land at the lake's northern end. The first lean-to you encounter on the western side is sited so that the sun will strike into it during the morning and early afternoon, so it is a good place to stop for lunch.

On your return try skiing down the brook, starting on the left, or east, bank. You are now between the brook and the trail, so no matter which way you go you will be led to their convergence at the bridge you crossed on the way in. You can set your own trail as the marsh opens up, picking your route as you choose. Be alert for the beaver houses and other signs of wildlife as you move through here, and go quietly so as to minimize any disturbance to the area.

You pick up the trail again at the bridge. Enjoy a downhill run back to Mill Brook. Once there, it is level going back to your car.

10 Crane Pond

Distance: 4½ miles (one-way)
Map: USGS 15' Paradox Lake
Two hills with moderate grades

The Pharaoh Lake Wilderness Area is special in that there are many access points to its interconnecting trails; you can start at one access, ski through the area, and come out at another. In the northwest corner of this area, three of these accesses are within 1½, 3, and 4 miles respectively of Crane Pond, the site of a nineteenth-century sawmill and a sizable community long since abandoned. Although the tour described here is a through route past the pond, requiring that you be met at the far end, several other trips in the area are possible, among them simple in-and-out treks along the accesses mentioned here.

The preferred route to Crane Pond starts on the south side of NY 74 near Paradox Lake and goes 3 miles to the western or outlet end of Crane Pond. It then follows the unplowed Crane Pond Road for 1½ miles to a parking area for a total distance of 4½ miles. This trip is all over land and does not involve any travel over frozen bodies of water.

Another approach utilizes Tub Mill Marsh, a long narrow marsh at the northeastern end of Crane Pond, and does involve skiing over the frozen surface of Crane Pond. Here you would start or end at the third access, which is on NY 74 near Eagle Lake (see Tour 11). There are some fine outlooks from the pond so an excursion out on the lake is well worth the effort regardless of how you come in. The distance from NY 74 at the Eagle Lake access is 2 miles to Tub Mill Marsh, and from the marsh to and across Crane Pond another 2 miles.

Driving directions start from Exit 28 on I-87 just north of Schroon Lake. Leaving I-87, cross US 9, and take NY 74 east towards Ticonderoga. The best parking will be just before you reach the trailhead. In 3.7 miles watch for a series of summer camps and boarding houses on the left. The first is called Idlewilde and has an Amoco gas pump in its snowed-in parking area. There will then be a white painted summer boarding house, and just beyond, a summer tourist camp with a blue "phone" sign hanging near the road. Park along the roadside in the vicinity of these structures. Just ahead you will see a speed limit sign and warning for a

Lunch on the shore of Crane Pond

left-hand turn. Walk to these signs and 200 feet beyond
them look on the right, or south, side of the road for
the Department of Environmental Conservation (DEC)
signboard directing you to Crane Pond.

(You will also want directions to the parking lot on
Crane Pond Road where the tour ends. Starting again
at Exit 28 on I-87, drive to US 9, parallel to and only a
few feet east on I-87. Follow US 9 south for.6 miles to
Alder Meadow Road on the left (east). In .5 mile you
pass the town landfill on the right and forest ranger
headquarters on the left. The road will fork in 1.9
miles; a yellow sign on the left indicates Crane Pond
Road, which ends in the parking lot. The right-hand
fork is the East Shore Road. To reach this second
entrance coming from the village of Schroon Lake,
drive north from town on US 9 for a little less than 2
miles and turn right (east) on Alder Meadow Road.)

The trail was at one time an old logging road and later
was used as a snowmobile route, so it is a good width.
It starts on an easy upgrade, reaching a notch under
Blue Hill in just over ¾ mile. Then follows a sharp,
short descent into a marshy area set about with huge
hemlocks. You skirt the edge of the bog for ¼ mile and
then begin a climb of some 300 vertical feet over an
unnamed rise of ground. The top of this rise is 2 miles
from the start. There now is a 200-vertical-foot drop,
some of it of considerably steep, to the unplowed Crane
Pond Road. Directly before you is Alder Pond, which is
really a westerly extension of Crane Pond. The site of
the old sawmill is ½ mile to your left, or the east.

These forests were vigorously cut over in the late nineteenth century, and the old sawmill was active from
about 1850-1910. The remains of the old dam and the
turbine that powered the mill were visible until 1950

and there is still a low dam at this site today. Originally the dam was significantly higher and Crane Pond was greatly enlarged from its present size.

The old route from Schroon Lake to Ticonderoga came up the Crane Pond Road, continued around the southern shore, then went past Rock Pond to pick up the old iron workings there, then overland to Chilson, and thence to Ticonderoga. Look at your map and note the stream entering Crane Pond that drains the Glidden Marsh to the south. A large settlement existed there in the middle nineteenth century. It was not just a shanty town, for cellar holes up to thirty by fifty feet can be discovered there. Exploration must wait until summer, however, for the ruins are now buried under the snow. These communities depended on logging and on the iron ore workings, both of which were depleted about the turn of this century.

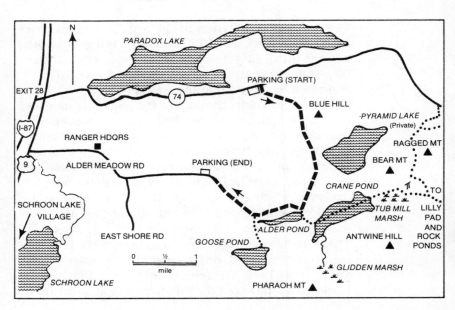

The loggers of that period cut what they wanted, leaving the rest to pile up as it would, and so mounds of treetops and branches lay drying and withering all over this territory in the early 1900s. In 1915 these piles of logging slash caught fire. Pharaoh Mountain, Treadway Mountain, Peaked Hill, Bear Mountain, and Potter Mountain were engulfed in flames. The fire destroyed the soil, and the residue washed into the valleys in the rains that followed. The white snowfields you see on the mountains around you cover the bare rock scars of that fire.

To go out along the Crane Pond Road, turn right. You will have Alder Pond on your left for almost 1 mile. At the west end of this pond you will also pass a side trail to Goose Pond on the left. Goose Pond is less than ½ mile away and is well worth a visit. The last ½ mile of Crane Pond Road is an almost continuous downhill run to the parking lot.

11 Rock Pond

Distance: 8 miles
Map: USGS 15' Paradox Lake
Interesting terrain, some hills; three lean-tos,
three ponds

Rock Pond is located within the Pharaoh Lake
Wilderness Area, a compact area that contains some
twenty-two ponded waters and almost as many small
mountains. The USGS map is essential when traveling
this country. Reference will be made to many of these
mountains as landmarks. The Pharaoh Lake area is on
the edge of the Adirondack uplift; the many block
faults here make the terrain more abrupt than much
of the more typical Adirondack country described in
this book. The route selected for this tour offers the
best approach to Rock Pond on cross-country skis, but
you do have to go over a pass between Ragged
Mountain and Bear Mountain where there are some
significant hills.

The starting point for driving directions is Exit 28 off
I-87 just north of Schroon Lake. Turn to the east on NY
74 to Ticonderoga. Clock off a distance of 7.4 miles,
when you will pass between stone roadside pillars
indicating the boundary for the town of Ticonderoga.
Only .2 mile beyond, a large Department of Environmental Conservation (DEC) sign shows the trails to
the Tub Mill Marsh lean-to and a long list of other
objectives. In summer, you would normally take the
hiking trail that starts here, but it involves a very steep
climb. We recommend that you attempt a less well-
marked but flatter trail that lies .6 mile to the east.

The highway goes over a low rise and curves to the left so you see the end of Eagle Lake dead ahead. The best parking is where the road straightens out, on the side away from the lake. You have overshot the start of the trail somewhat, so walk or ski back along the road to the end of the steel highway guard rail. There is no sign where the trail starts, but the location is precisely pinpointed by a green highway marker numbered 74-2102-1125. Looking down the highway embankment

The snowfields on Peaked Hill covering rock bared in the 1915 fire are clearly visible from the Tub Mill Marsh

you see the dam across the outlet of Eagle Lake and the footbridge over it. Directly beyond the dam the unmarked trail, an old woods road, will bend slowly to the right. Head for the trail; now you are on your way.

Almost exactly 1 mile from NY 74 you will intersect the summer hiking trail, which is marked with blue DEC trail disks. The right-hand fork goes to NY 74, while straight ahead the trail enters the lands of a private camp on Pyramid Lake. Take the left-hand fork and drop down a short hill. The trail curves to the right as it goes under the cliffs of Ragged Mountain and then bends to the left. A climb of 300 vertical feet brings you to the pass between Ragged Mountain and Bear Mountain.

After 1/3 mile of fairly level going the trail curves to the left and starts downhill. You are near the edge of Tub Mill Marsh so the trail feels the west wind that blows up the marsh through the Rock Pond Brook valley. The snow may be windblown here. The drop is only 100 vertical feet, but it is a snappy grade nonetheless.

About the time your skis come to rest you will see a sign pointing to the right to the Tub Mill Marsh lean-to, which is almost within sight. To continue, keep straight ahead, following the blue trail markers to the crossing of Rock Pond Brook. This will require a snow bridge, or, if the brook is open, a short excursion downstream to the Tub Mill Marsh, which should bring you out on solid footing to get across. If you wish to go further down the marsh, you will see the cliffs on Bear Mountain to the northwest, while behind you can see the ice- and snow-covered rock slides on Peaked Hill. These are the scars of the 1915 fire. The USGS map will keep you oriented. Tub Mill Marsh is a northeast extension of Crane Pond, described in Tour 10.

With the crossing of Rock Pond Brook behind you, you start up a side slope of Pine Hill in a generally southeast direction. Honey Pond is just at the top of the rise and ½ mile from the Rock Pond Brook crossing. (If the trail is well packed, it will be a zippy ride on the way back.) It is a tiny body of water, but you will get a good view over it of the bare rock slides of Peaked Hill.

In another ¼ mile you come to Lilypad Pond; here you will encounter a signboard that shows the blue-marked trail continuing south to Horseshoe, Crab, and

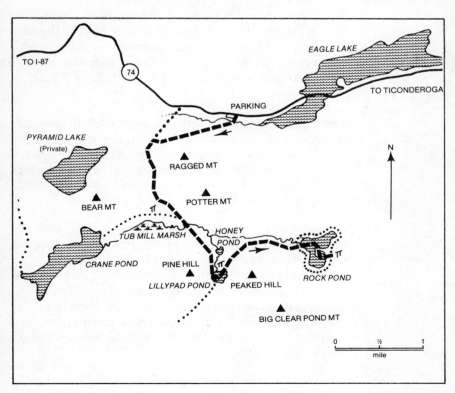

Oxshoe ponds. A red-marked trail goes left to Rock Pond only 1½ miles distant. Note the change from blue markers to red. If you turn at this junction, following the red hiking trail markers, you must cross the outlet of Lilypad Pond, which presents an awkward descent down one bank and a climb up the other. Our preferred route—for winter adventurers only—is to ski out on the pond, go about halfway down the left-hand, or north, shore and head inland through some plantation pines. Here, about 200 feet from the pond, there is a lean-to, which the red-marked trail to Rock Pond passes right by.

From here, this trail is wide and fairly level. It edges the base of Peaked Hill, swinging gradually more to the east. You pass a very small marshy pond on the left where you can look up at the great cliffs of Potter Mountain to the northwest. You are now within ½ mile of Rock Pond.

The trail circles Rock Pond, but if you wish to stop at the lean-to on the eastern shore, ski across the lake. This location gives a fine view of Peaked Hill, which has so much bare rock that it almost looks like a ski resort. We've been tempted to try these open slopes, but have not actually done it—yet.

The return is the same way you came in. If the idea of exploring this area further in winter intrigues you, we have one bit of advice, garnered from personal experience. The idea of developing a through trip from Lilypad Pond to Horseshoe Pond and thence to Crane Pond via the blue trail is appealing. Here the USGS map may let you down, for the contours as printed give no warning of how steep this trail really is, so we suggest that you stay off it.

12 Hoffman Notch

Distance: 10 miles
Map: USGS 15' Schroon Lake
Outstanding wilderness tour; moderately difficult grades

Most of the wilderness area ski tours in this guide are forested routes to ponds and lakes. Hoffman Notch is a deep and narrow opening between Washburn Ridge and Texas Ridge with cliffs, ice falls, and rugged scenery. Near the tour's highest point there is a pond and marshy area, which permits a clear, fine view of Texas Ridge.

The trip is especially appealing because it provides the opportunity for either a through trip between two roads or a one-way, in-and-out tour. The Wills Run Ski Touring Center is close by, and parties can make arrangements with the center to start at the northern end and ski through the notch to the southern terminus, where they will be met and driven to their car. For more information, contact the Wills Run Ski Touring Center, Hoffman Road, Schroon Lake, New York 12870 (phone: 518-532-7936).

The route described here was a snowmobile trail until the area was designated as a wilderness, so all stream crossings from the southern end to the notch are well bridged. This makes the tour attractive for late spring skiing, when meltouts and fast water from spring runoff can close other trails.

This trip will start at the southern end, bring you to Big Marsh, where the best views are to be had, and

then take you up into the notch to the height-of-land.
While we indicate how to find the northern terminus of
the route, we do not describe it. Those planning a
through trip should be highly experienced wilderness
skiers.

To reach the starting point, drive to the village of
Schroon Lake, which lies between Exits 27 and 28 on
I-87. From the southern end of town, turn west onto
Hoffman Road, which climbs steadily as it leaves the
lake. You pass the Wills Run Ski Touring Center in 3.3
miles and Essex County 24B, which leaves left for
Olmsteadville, in 4.8 miles. Continue past Potash Road,
at 5.4 miles, and turn right onto Loch Muller Road at

The Hoffman Notch brook

6.4 miles. The road ends in a parking area; the great white pine tree you see was planted as a seedling here in 1845.

You'll have a view through the notch from the parking area. Texas Ridge, the notch's right-hand wall, is actually a spur of the larger Blue Ridge, whose highest point, Hoffman Mountain, dominates the landscape to the right. Looking through the notch you can see the sharp protuberance of the Hornet Cobbles, poking up from the notch floor.

The trail leaves in front of a blue house with white trim and drops to the outlet of Bailey Pond. It then climbs the lower slopes of Washburn Ridge and levels out to contour along a side slope. Watch for a trail 1¾ miles from the start. A former snowmobile trail marked for Big Roger Pond, which the USGS map shows as Big Pond, departs to the right. This route involves considerable climbing over the end of Texas Ridge and is not recommended for skiers.

You will then pick up the brook called North Branch on the USGS map and follow it steadily up through a small notch that contains many boulders dropped by a glacier long ago. You will be through this notch 2½ miles from the start, and the grade will begin to level off. In another ½ mile the terrain will beome almost flat, an indication that you are approaching Big Marsh, and the view will start to open up. The best panoramas on the tour are from the marsh itself, which you reach in another ½ mile. The peak that dominates the landscape to the southeast is the southern part of Texas Ridge; it hides Hoffman Mountain from view.

Beyond Big Marsh you will be traveling through a group of black birch, an unusual tree for this altitude,

and about 4 miles from your start, the sides of the
notch will close in. Stay close to the brook (we could
not locate the trail on the USGS map that appears to
edge the side of the Hornet Cobbles). For the next mile
you will see the ice cliffs on Washburn Ridge to the
west and sense the precipitous slope of the Hornet
Cobbles above you.

The turn-around point for the trip is where the trail
starts to descend in a shelving manner, with sharp
drops and level stretches in succession. The grade gets
steeper the further you go once you pass the height-
of-land.

For those who want to make a through trip starting
from the north, take I-87 to Exit 29, and drive west on

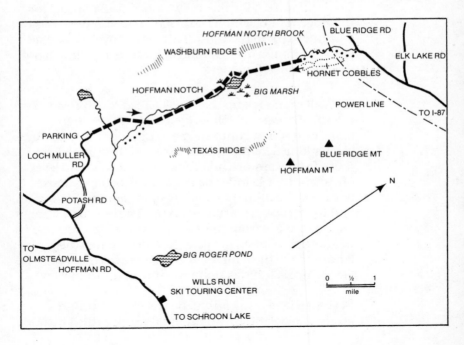

Boreas Road towards Blue Ridge. In about 4 miles you will pass Elk Lake Road on the right. Continue for another .5 mile and look for a pole meant to hold a hanging sign. The road dips to cross The Branch watercourse near the start of the trail. The USGS map shows the trail departing due south, but it has been rerouted to go to the southeast before swinging around to the south. From this point on, the USGS sheet is entirely adequate for those who know what they are doing, and persons who need highly detailed directions should not attempt such an ambitious trip.

The outstanding features of the northern approach are the huge boulders that have toppled off the upper slopes of both Washburn Ridge and the Hornet Cobbles. Some of these seem as big as a house. You should also know that because the northern section runs on an easement through private land the stream crossings are not bridged, so this half of the route may not be reliable in the late spring.

The Hoffman Notch ski tour is the outstanding trip in this guide in terms of a variety of rugged mountain scenery. To take advantage of this requires the stamina to engage in a 10-mile trip. The opportunity to combine this with a through trip for the highly experienced makes it even more attractive. We anticipate many more ski tracks in Hoffman Notch in the coming years.

13 Camp Dippikill

Distance: 5 miles (one-way)
Map: USGS 15' North Creek
Moderate to steep downhill sections; beaver colony

In the early days of skiing in the United States, before
ski lifts were invented, cross-country skiing meant
exploring favorite summer hiking trails, and a fast
downhill run on a narrow twisting trail was an important part of the adventure. Today, the kick-and-glide
motion of cross-country skiing emphasizes trails with
rather easy ups-and-downs and long run-outs, so there
is little demand placed on Alpine skiing skills.

This trip is definitely geared to those for whom the fast
downhill ride is of the essence. It is a through trip that
starts with a relatively easy 2-mile loop at about the
1,800-foot level and then sweeps downhill to end at
about 750 feet. Camp Dippikill is not recommended for
flatland skiers, as all its trails have some hills. As the
suggested start is close to the highest point of land,
you will encounter a downhill section no matter which
route you take. The downgrades closest to the top are
not particularly challenging, but those with limited
downhill experience would better enjoy a flatter area.

These trails are found on a tract of land owned by the
Student Association of the State University of New
York at Albany. This area is open to the public for day
use. There are lean-tos, closed cabins, and other facil-
ities for overnight use, but these are reserved for the
students, faculty, and staff of the university. All visitors

are required to register at the Camp Dippikill office on
arrival and are directed to an assigned parking area.
Students of the State University at Albany also have
overnight privileges at the Glen House, a youth hostel,
where this tour ends.

One of the attractive objectives in this area is Dippikill
Pond, which is set about with hemlocks and spruce
and which hosts a beaver colony. Their dam and house
are at the pond's northeastern end.

A particularly fine way to tour Camp Dippikill is to
gather a party large enough to require at least two
automobiles, one of which will be left at the Glen
House. After exploring the trails at the top, you can all
meet for lunch at the lean-to by Dippikill Pond. As
many as desire can then plunge down the mountain to
the Glen House, while those who are less dashing can
return to the start by a variety of routes.

To reach the Dippikill area from Warrensburg, proceed
north on US 9 to the intersection of NY 28, on the left
about 2 miles from town. You cross the Hudson River
on NY 28 in 5 miles and almost immediately pass the
Glen House, formerly an old logging camp, on the left.
About .2 mile beyond the river crossing, Glen Creek
Road departs to the left through a picturesque valley.
Follow it, climbing continuously, until you reach
Dippikill Pond Road on the left at 1.3 miles. There is a
sign for the camp at this corner. Slightly less than 1
mile up the road you pass the first parking lot; pull off
to the left at the second clearing and check in at the
Camp Dippikill office. A tall steel tower with a wind-
generator stands directly above this building; it is the
area's electric power supply.

You are now ready to ski. Starting near the base of the
tower, an unnamed service trail leads parallel to the

road. Head south on the gentle upgrade. In about ⅜ mile the trail veers to the right to the road, where there is a white-painted house, a small parking lot, and two privies. Cross the road and turn to the right on a trail marked with a blue snowflake on a disk. On this loop you will encounter first a series of downgrades and then a succession of climbs past some of the cabins built by the Student Association. You will return to Dippikill Pond Road after a trip of about 2 miles.

The route we've chosen to the lunch spot on Dippikill Pond involves the easiest downhill grades. Turn to the right, or south, and either ski the top of the plow bank or walk along the road. You come to the ski trail on the left in about ⅜ mile. The drop over the first 50 feet or so is the steepest grade in the 1-mile distance to the pond.

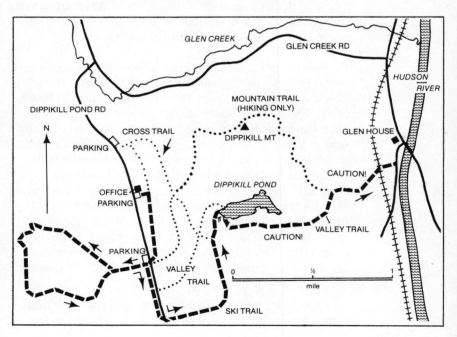

The accompanying map shows other routes that have more exciting downhill possibilities.

Once you've explored the pond and the beaver works—and taken a bite of lunch—you can decide whether to continue all the way down the mountain. The trail loses 500 feet over about a mile, but most of this is taken in two drops with a more gentle section intervening. This trail is fast, make no mistake about it. If the snow holds either a breakable or unbreakable crust, we'd suggest climbing back to the road. On one visit to this area when there was a breakable crust covered with about four inches of powder snow, a group of dauntless skiers attempted this run against better advice, and they came out at the Glen House showing cuts where they had crashed face-down in the fragmented crust.

Under good snow conditions, though, it is a delightful run for those who can handle it, and you may want to do it more than once if you can make transportation arrangements. In fact, in this day and age when we are all trying to become less dependent on gas-based transportation and hoping to cultivate more personal reliance, you might consider making this a circuit tour, starting and ending at the bottom by the Glen House. The route is really not difficult to climb. Try it; you'll like it!

14 Second Pond

Distance: 6½ miles
Map: USGS 15' Thirteenth Lake
Easy to moderate grades; blazed wilderness trail

Although many people talk romantically of blazing a trail into unknown territory, few today have had to depend on old-time blazed markers to find their way into the Adirondack wilderness. The trail you follow to Second Pond, in the Siamese Ponds Wilderness Area, gives you a chance to try your hand at reading these route markers of old.

Here you will ski through some tall timber, maples and yellow birches that rise fifty to seventy feet to the first branch. The feeling of wilderness is maintained at the tour's destination, Second Pond. Three-quarters of a mile long with a small island in its center, it is set about with hemlock and spruce. From the pond, you can look up at the bulk of Gore Mountain, whose upper slopes are scarred with cliffs.

The trail you will follow was originally a logging road blazed by woodsmen in the nineteenth century. The word "blaze" comes from the French *blesser*, to wound, and refers to the scar that results from chopping out a piece of bark about as big as a man's hand to expose the white sapwood of the tree. In time, the tree attempts to close over this wound so that scar tissue, distinctly different from the bark, envelops the old blaze. These are the marks you must recognize.

To reach this tour's start, travel to the hamlet of
Wevertown at the intersection of NY 8 and NY 28. From
Wevertown, follow NY 8 southwest 3.2 miles to Chatiemac Road, on the right. The green New York State
highway markers also reference this junction. When
coming from Wevertown, the last marker before
Chatiemac Road is numbered 8/1710/1133. If you are
coming from the other direction, look for marker
8/1710/1132, which is directly opposite the turnoff.
Chatiemac Road winds around the shores of Ross Lake
and then climbs a long hill, gaining about 600 feet of
elevation. Be sure to have your snow tires. The
trailhead is an unmarked but well-defined opening in
the trees on the right 2.2 miles from NY 8. Because it is
easy to overshoot, note these additional landmarks.
The "No Trespassing" posters of the Chatiemac Club
are nailed to trees just beyond the trailhead. If you
prefer not to turn your car around here, continue
about .8 mile and turn at the entrance to the Chatiemac Club, a private hunting and fishing club. Approaching from this direction, you will see a yellow New
York State Forest Preserve poster where the Chatiemac
Club posters stop. This is the boundary of state land.
The trail is 80 feet beyond, and the roadside parking is
better on the trail side of the road.

Since this trail is not maintained by the state and has
no signs or trail markers, you should carry a topo-
graphic map and a compass, and be aware of your
position at all times. The old blazes are sufficiently
frequent so that a few minutes of travel should take
you from one to another. If you miss a blaze, turn back
until you find one (they are on both sides of a tree), and
then leave one of your party at this point while others
spread out casting about for the next.

*You follow blazes—scars like this one on a tree's trunk—on
the trail to Second Pond.*

Shoulder your day pack, and head off on the trail into a
mixed forest of spruce, hemlock, and hardwood. You
cross the outlet of Chatiemac Lake in about ¼ mile.
If you are early in the season and the outlet is imper-
fectly frozen but the lake is quite solid, you can make a
short detour out onto the lake to get by. The trail then
climbs gently, and down to the right you can see a vly
or swampy area on Black Brook, while straight ahead
the slopes of Gore Mountain show through the trees.
About 2/3 mile from the start, after going over a
height-of-land, dropping down a short grade, and
crossing a gully that comes in from the left, the trail
abruptly changes direction. Bearing sharply left, it
climbs a ridge parallel to the gully. The compass
heading going up this slope is 340 degrees magnetic.
Note also that on your return you'll be going down this

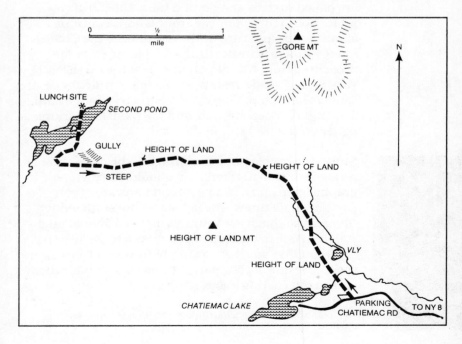

slope and then turning sharply at the bottom; if you fail to make the turn, you must fall to avoid the trees, so take the time now to stamp out the snow at this corner to make it easier to negotiate. This is the only spot that entails any technical skiing problems.

It is at the top of this rise, 2/3 mile from the gully, that you encounter the tall timber and the big trees that make this stretch so beautiful. The nineteenth-century lumbermen only wanted the softwoods, spruce for the most part, and so they left the maples, beeches, and yellow birches. The beeches have been affected by a fungus so that the maples and birches have become dominant. If your camera will accept a wide-angle lense, this is the place to use it.

The descent through the hardwood forest lasts about 4/10 mile. The trail then levels out and enters a hemlock and spruce grove. There is a slight dip followed by a second upgrade ¼ mile long. Beyond this rise, the trail drops on the steepest section of the tour. When the terrain levels out again, you should begin to catch glimpses of Second Pond through the big hemlocks and spruces. The trail continues on for another 1/10 mile or so, and then swings toward your destination in a right-hand, downhill U-turn that brings you to the pond's edge, roughly 3¼ miles from your start. The small island will be directly before you.

The best lunch spot of Second Pond is diagonally across from you. To reach it, skirt the island on your left-hand side. There is a cove on the opposite shore with a small clearing used as a camping spot by summer fishermen. The sun strikes in this opening, while the thick spruce growth shelters it from the wind.

The journey back is every bit as fine as the trek out.

15 John Pond

Distance: 4 miles
Map: USGS 15' Thirteenth Lake
Easy grades, a scenic wilderness pond

The tour to John Pond, on the northwest edge of the
Siamese Ponds Wilderness Area, is a delightful, easy
trip in the heart of the Adirondacks. It doesn't involve
much climbing on the way in, but you gain enough
height so that there are several pleasant downhill runs
coming out. Because the route follows a jeep road, the
trail is wide enough to allow two people to travel
abreast if the snow surface cooperates. There is a lean-
to at the pond, and the shoreline is rugged, with some
prominent outcrops and small cliffs on a rise of ground
to the northwest.

You approach the trail from back roads to the south
and east of the village of Indian Lake. From the junction of NY 28 and NY 30 in Indian Lake, head south on
NY 30 to Big Brook Road, on the left (east) by the
Indian Lake Motel and Restaurant. Follow Big Brook
Road, crossing the upper end of Indian Lake on a
causeway, for 2.4 miles to Chamberlain Road, which
comes in from the left. Bear right to stay on Big Brook
Road, following the sign for the Chimney Mountain
Craftsmen. One mile from Chamberlain Road you
reach a cluster of homes and trailers and the workshop
of the Chimney Mountain Craftsmen. The road forks;
bear left toward the Rainbow Club, whose gated
entrance you pass in .8 mile. The road surface turns to
gravel here; just beyond you come to a T-junction, bear

Looking up from the John Pond lean-to to the cliffs made visible by one of the great fires

right again and drive the short distance to a parking area at the road's end. Straight ahead is an Adirondack vly or wetland, while the trail itself, marked here with a metal maroon-painted sign with a white arrow, departs to the left.

Although there are only a few trail markers along the route, the jeep road is easy to follow. At ½ mile you pass another vly, across which you can see Snowy Mountain and other peaks on the far side of Indian Lake. At 1 1/10 miles you reach a trail junction that is potentially confusing. Here the jeep road to John Pond makes a sharp left turn. The route you are following shows as an opening in a scrub forest; it climbs an upgrade perhaps 50 feet long and then enters an open field. (If you miss this turn and continue straight on the trail to Puffer Pond, you will climb for about 20 feet, pass a big fir tree, and then drop down to stay in the forest.)

Beyond the clearing the trail rises through a spruce-fir forest by a series of gentle upgrades, none of which are at all steep. You soon begin to pass to the left of a meadow, across which you have a good view of the Bullhead Mountain Range. Skiing along the meadow's edge, you come, at 1½ miles, to a grove of big white pines, where the trail swings to the north and heads for John Pond.

Shortly you encounter a sign that reads "John Pond 0.5 miles," but according to our estimates, the actual distance is closer to 1/3 mile. Here another jeep road goes off to the right, but it only leads a short way to a clearing where hunters make camp.

The last leg to John Pond is through red pine and spruce, a woods that has the appearance of being reforested. Later on, you will see other evidence of the severe forest fires that swept this area in the early twentieth century.

There is a lean-to at the south end of the pond, where the trail emerges from the woods 2 miles from its start. In this location, the shelter is exposed to any northwest wind. The day we were out, there was no wind, so we ate our lunch here. But on a cold windy day with no sun, it is better to retreat into the woods to gain some shelter if you're planning to stop to eat. If the day is bright, but with a northwest wind, the far end of the pond offers a lee.

The cliffs and ledges that rise on the western side of the pond show the effects of past abuses to the land. The logging industry ethic of the nineteenth and early twentieth centuries was one of cut, let burn, and get out, and companies often let land they had already logged revert to the state for non-payment of taxes. The lumbermen took what they wanted, mostly softwoods for paper pulp, and left the tops and the branches lying as they fell. These residues were supported off the ground so they did not rot, but baked in the sun and dried in the wind to a state of explosive inflammability. The lumbermen called this "slash."

When the spark came, as sooner or later it did, these tinder dry branches burned with such intensity that the organic matter in the soil beneath was destroyed. The rains that followed washed the life-supporting soil away, leaving bare rock outcrops that will require ages to revegetate. You see above you the result of one such burn.

If you go out on the frozen lake, you will notice to the south a mountain with a curious spire sticking up on one side. This is the chimney of Chimney Mountain. It

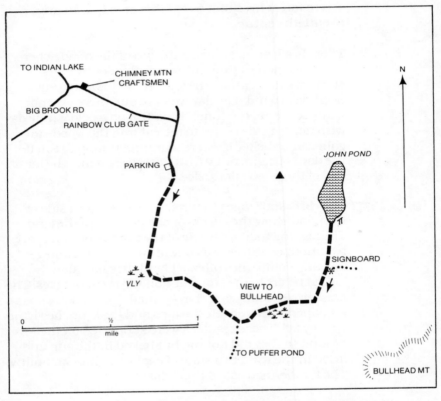

is an intrusion of igneous rock more resistant to weathering than the formation into which it penetrated. Today it remains, while the surrounding material has weathered away. There are caves in Chimney Mountain where the ice persists all year long.

When you are ready, return the way you came. Going out, the trip is fast and pleasant. There is a continuous loss of altitude all the way, resulting in a series of downhill runs that are pleasant but not so fast as to be unmanageable.

16 Stephens and Cascade Ponds

Distance: 7 miles
Map: USGS 15' Blue Mountain
Adirondack bushwhack; steep downhill stretches

Both Stephens Pond and Cascade Pond are small bodies of water set in a mountain landscape. Both have Adirondack lean-tos on their shores. Stephens Pond is directly on the Northville-Placid Trail, while Cascade Pond is 1½ miles away on a spur trail.

As you can see on the accompanying sketch map, the Northville-Placid Trail does not take the most direct route from NY 28/30 to Stephens Pond. It happens to follow logging roads, and the loggers pushed their road directly into Cascade Pond, not to Stephens, climbing over a shoulder of an unnamed mountain that we, for convenience, call Hill 2407. From this height-of-land they then dropped a road down to Stephens Pond. Because this stretch includes a right-angle bend in the steepest section, it is good to climb on skis but not safe to descend.

To avoid this problem, our route takes a shortcut by map and compass directly through the Adirondack forest from the Northville-Placid Trail to Stephens Pond. A triangular circuit is thus created in the middle of the tour. Navigation by map and compass is called bushwhacking in these parts, but this particular bushwhack is only ¼ mile long, and it follows well-defined natural features. If you are just beginning to become familiar with the use of map and compass you will find this tour a good beginning exercise.

The tour starts where the Northville-Placid Trail crosses NY 28/30 about 8 miles west of the village of Indian Lake and 2 miles east of the hamlet of Blue Mountain Lake. There is a forest ranger's headquarters about 1,000 feet east of the crossing, which is easily identified by a parking area and large signboard for the trail on the south side of the highway.

Initially the Northville-Placid Trail follows roads in the Lake Durant public campsite, on the shore of Lake Durant directly south of NY 28/30. You will start to the

A springtime lunch before the Stephens Pond lean-to

south on a campsite road that angles generally to the
left, or east. Within ¼ mile you will cross a bridge over
the Rock River, the outlet to Lake Durant, which is now
on your right. Just below the bridge, turn to the right
at a T-junction with a second campsite road, and follow
a sign marked "Trail." The campsite road follows the
shore of Lake Durant, going first southwest and then
west. The Northville-Placid Trail then departs to the left
at a second sign marked "Trail." You climb gently for
¾ mile and then encounter a level section for another
¾ mile.

Now you should look for the point to begin the
bushwhack route. Hunters and fishermen have
marked some secret symbols on trees near the logical
spot. Watch the right-hand side of the trail for a small
maple where there are two X marks carved in the bark.
A few trees further on you should spot an inverted L
done in red paint, above which a blue trail marker has
been nailed. About 200 feet farther watch for a faded
red bull's eye about four inches in diameter. This is the
critical mark. If you overshoot this one, you will quickly
start a definite ascent over a shoulder of Hill 2407.

About 50 feet beyond the bull's eye you may see an
opening on the left where some fishermen have clipped
out a trail to Stephens Pond, and occasionally a ranger
goes in here too and packs out a track on snowshoes.
In any event look for a good place to leave the trail to
the left. Set your compass for a bearing of 230 degrees
magnetic. You will be going parallel to the shoulder of
Hill 2407, which you will be able to see through the
trees. By keeping this rise of ground in sight and
checking your compass, you should come out on the
pond, not more than ¼ mile distant. If you have been
going in the woods for more than twenty minutes and
you have discovered no sign of the pond, perhaps it

would be best to retrace your track to the main trail.
However, since many people have reached Stephens
Pond with far less elaborate directions, we anticipate
few problems. Once you get out on the lake, it is about
¾ mile down to the lean-to, which is on the right or
west side. In an attractive setting of hemlocks and
hardwoods, it is a well-sheltered spot to have lunch.

The Northville-Placid Trail going north leaves from the
rear of the lean-to and proceeds directly toward the
steep flank of Hill 2407. It then angles sharply right
and follows an old logging road that is cut into the side
of the hill. At the top of this ascent, the trail swings to
the left, or west, and climbs less steeply for a ways. A

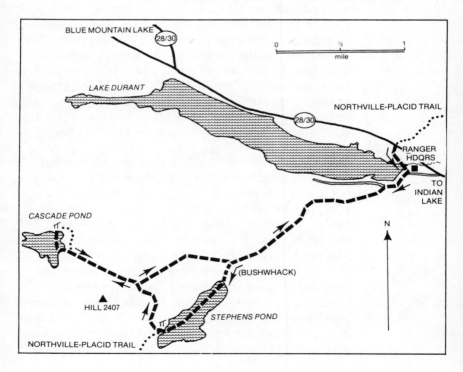

steeper ascent follows and then ½ mile from Stephens Pond you come to a trail junction well marked with signboards. If you were following the Northville-Placid Trail north, you would turn sharply right at this point, as indicated by the signs. The trail to Cascade Pond goes straight ahead.

The trail to Cascade Pond, now only 1 mile away, is very wide, so that the downhill run you encounter almost at once is a real joy. At the bottom you will see an opening through the trees that looks like the pond, but it is only a frozen-over marsh. Continuing for another ¼ mile will bring you in view of an arm of the pond.

It may be preferable at this point to go through the woods and out onto the pond. By skirting the eastern shore you will come to the lean-to in a little cove at the pond's extreme northeastern corner. While the trail does continue beyond the lean-to to the west and north, it becomes excessively steep in spots and is not recommended to skiers.

To return retrace your steps to the signboards at the height-of-land. Take what is now the left-hand or north fork and follow the Northville-Placid Trail along the old logging road back to Lake Durant and the highway.

17 Tirrell Pond

Distance: 6 2/3 miles
Map: USGS 15' Blue Mountain
Moderate ups-and-downs; narrow trail,
intermediate skiing skill required

In 1922 the newly formed Adirondack Mountain Club
conceived of a long-distance footpath that would
traverse the Adirondack Mountains. Private automobiles had not come into general use at that time,
and the roads in the Adirondack region were little
more than dirt tracks. A southern starting point of
Northville was selected because an inter-urban trolley
line had its northern terminus at this town. There was
rail service from Utica to the village of Lake Placid, so
that both ends of the proposed 130-mile-long wilderness trail were accessible by public transportation.

While most of the trail was completed by the late
1920s, one gap remained, that between Tirrell Pond
and the village of Long Lake. In 1932 and 1933 Almy
had summer jobs working on the trail crew that
completed this remaining section. The base camp for
this operation was established on the east shore of
Tirrell Pond right under the great cliffs that rise on
Tirrell Mountain.

Land ownership in this part of the Adirondacks
consists of small parcels of state land interspersed
with private holdings, and the trail passes through
both. Because wilderness areas are required to be
larger continuous tracts, the state land here is
classified only as wild forest. This legal designation

does not detract from the wilderness quality. The trail winds up and down over small bumps and twists about to avoid destroying major trees. The combination of continually climbing and falling and many turns means that some skiing skill is needed.

There are two Adirondack open-faced lean-tos at Tirrell Pond, one at the south end and one at the north. These

A striking view of Blue Mountain on the approach to Tirrell Pond

are 3 1/3 and 4¼ miles from NY 28 respectively, so this area is popular with winter campers. You stand a good chance of finding a packed-out track, which will make for easier skiing.

The Northville-Placid Trail crosses NY 28 about 8 miles west of the village of Indian Lake and 2 miles east of the hamlet of Blue Mountain Lake. There is a plowed parking area on the south side of the highway near the crossing, which is 1,000 feet or so west of the local forest ranger headquarters, a low building on the south side of the road. The Department of Environmental Conservation (DEC) forest rangers maintain offices in their homes, and this force of dedicated outdoorsmen are glad to be of assistance in advising on trail conditions in their territories. (This is the same parking area used in Tour 16.)

There is a highway cut here at the crossing, and the trail sign is on top of the bank at the edge of the woods. The cut is steep so ascend it on a long traverse.

Once in the woods heading north you will discover a series of short climbs and descents leading to a climb over a low height-of-land ½ mile in. Then follows an easy descent to the crossing of O'Neil Flow, a flat marshy area. In the old days a flow meant a flat area just covered with water so "the water flowed over the ground." Flows can be created either by natural causes or by old logging dams. The main extent of O'Neil Flow is to the east, so that you only cross a small arm of the main body. Just before reaching the flow, the climax forest environment will change abruptly, and until you come close to Tirrell Pond you will be crossing the lands of a private paper company. Portions of this area were logged off at various times in the past, and the skid roads and haul roads still exist, although they are somewhat overgrown. The ranger makes it a point to

keep this part of the trail well marked with the blue
DEC trail disks.

The point at which you enter paper company land and
encounter the O'Neil Flow is about 1 mile from NY 28.
Looking across the flow you will see a shoulder of Blue
Mountain. The trail will skirt the eastern edge of this
obstruction and consequently will veer to the right.
The trail will resume its northly direction about 1½
miles from the start.

At this point the trail will cross a small stream, which
may be hard to recognize under deep snow cover.

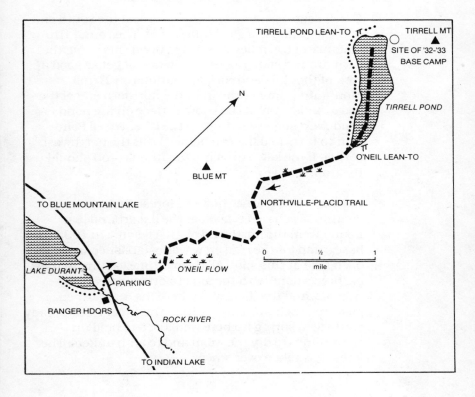

Having made this crossing you will find yourself
swinging more to the northwest, as you follow the
stream for perhaps ¼ mile. In summer there is wet
ground in this region so the trail makes a gradual
climb to gain firmer, drier ground. By the time you
have gone 2 miles, the trail will have worked its way
around the summer wet spot and resumed an almost
due north direction.

You will now have the pleasure of an easy downhill run
that lasts about ¼ mile. By this time you will have
completed 2½ miles of the trip to the end of the pond.
The last ½ mile or so is generally level going.

O'Neil Lean-to, named for the flow, is at the south end
of the lake and is a good lunch spot. The round-trip
distance of 6²/₃ miles was based upon this being the
turn-around spot. However, you do not get as good a
view of the cliffs and rock formations on Tirrell
Mountain from here as from the northern end of the
lake, 1 mile away. If the snow surface on the pond is
good, we'd suggest skiing up the lake. Tirrell Pond
lean-to is tucked in deep hemlocks at the northwest
corner. If the lake surface is unsuitable, you should use
the trail.

It is interesting to see how the forest environment
continually changes. Look at the flat ground just
inland from the north end of Tirrell Pond. In 1933 the
base camp for the trail crew was established in a sunny
open field at this spot. All the old-time logging in these
parts was done with the aid of horses instead of
tractors, and this field was where the lumbermen
pastured their animals. In 1933 the small trees already
starting to spring up here were used to hold up
clotheslines to dry the wash and to air blankets. The
forest has taken over since.

18 Cascade Lake

Distance: 5½ miles (or 2 miles)
Map: USGS 15' Big Moose
Easy grades, wilderness trip

The trail to Cascade Lake is ideal for beginning ski tourers. Leading roughly a mile to the foot of a most attractive lake which it then circles, it is very wide, well marked, and relatively level. The combination of a good objective close to the trailhead for novices and a longer loop for the more adventurous makes it a fine trip for a party of various ages and levels of ability.

These features arise because this route was a snow-mobile trail for a time prior to 1973, and a truck trail even earlier. If you passed through the Old Forge area, you undoubtedly became aware that Old Forge prides itself on being the snowmobile capital of the world. In the early days of this sport, about 1965, every possible woods route in this area was widened and bridged to make it suitable for snowmobiles, with no routes left solely for cross-country skiing. The 1972 policy of classifying certain parts of the Adirondacks as wilderness has the effect of closing these routes to motorized equipment. At that time an equivalent mileage of trails was added to wild forest lands to compensate for the loss to snowmobilers.

There are at least four Cascade Lakes in the Adiron-dacks: this one, the one just north of Eagle Bay on the Fulton Chain Lakes, and the ones off NY 73 in the High Peaks Region near Lake Placid. There is also a Cascade

Pond to the east on NY 28 near Blue Mountain Lake
(see Tour 16). To find the correct "Cascade" for this
tour follow NY 28 to the village of Eagle Bay, between
Old Forge and Racquette Lake. In the village, turn to
the northwest on Big Moose Road, which soon forks.
You can follow either road, as they merge again shortly.
About 200 feet beyond where the two roads come
together, and .9 mile from NY 28, a parking lot is
partially plowed out on the right-hand side of the road.
Leave your car here.

The official trailhead with a signboard, motor vehicle
barrier, and register booth is about 100 feet into the
woods on the right. Although you can proceed directly
to it, an old logging road about 100 feet back along Big
Moose Road offers an easier grade.

The trail starts on a gentle upgrade but soon levels off.
After about ten minutes travel, look to your left and you
will see an opening in the trees and a meadow beyond.
You are looking at and over the outlet of Cascade Lake.
As the meadow's northern and northwest sides are
thick evergreens, it is a fine place to get out of the wind
on a blustery day. Since this tour is a short one, you
might want to explore this area a bit sometime during
the day.

Now you come to an easy downgrade, but do not watch
the trail ahead so intently that you do not see the
yellow disk markers to the right that show where the
returning trail comes in. This junction is just before a
large clearing at the bottom of the hill.

You will skirt this clearing, hugging the southwestern
or left-hand side, and shortly cross a footbridge over
the outlet of Cascade Lake. Looking downstream you
see the continuation of the meadow you spotted

View from the footbridge on the Cascade Lake Trail

earlier. It is a pleasant vista and a good spot for some photography.

Just beyond the bridge, you will see signboards for trails to Queer Lake and Windfall Pond. There is some steep going on these, and they are not recommended to skiers.

The trail bends to the right, and Cascade Lake comes into view. You can explore it on the ice or go around by the trail. The west, or left-hand, side has a steep rise of ground, and the trail will hug the lakeshore at first. About halfway up the lake, you will climb. You come down near the upper end of the lake, which you then swing around, making a short climb and descent as you do. Once past the upper end of the lake, it is a straight shot down the eastern shore to pick up the incoming trail near the clearing you skied through on the way to Cascade Lake.

It is probably a good idea for those who are just starting wilderness skiing not to attempt the full trip around the lake. If others in your party want to try that loop, you might care to build a fire while you wait, if for no other reason than to develop some skill in this important survival art.

Look for some dead hardwood branches, such as beech or maple. They should have the bark coming off to show some bare dry wood. The softwoods like spruce do not release as much heat and don't burn down to coals. Find the most sheltered spot available, and if any wind is stirring, stamp out a spot in the snow with your skis to keep the fire out of the wind. Collect a bunch of junk wood to make a supporting raft on the snow so that you do not kindle the fire directly on the snow.

In your firewood supply find two sticks about the size
of a broom handle and lay one on the other to form a V
on top of the "raft." Now break up all the tiny twigs into
a bundle and pile them against the inside of the V so
they are sloping upwards. Sort the firewood you have
collected into pieces the size of toothpicks, spaghetti,
pencils, golf club shafts, broom handles, and baseball
bats. You can split or shave the smaller sticks with a
pocket knife to reduce them to the required fineness.
Put the match under the very finest twigs or shavings
first, and as these light put on the next largest pieces
and so on. Be sure to place them where the flames
will ignite them.

The first few minutes in the life of a winter campfire
are very touchy. Beginners at fire-building usually do

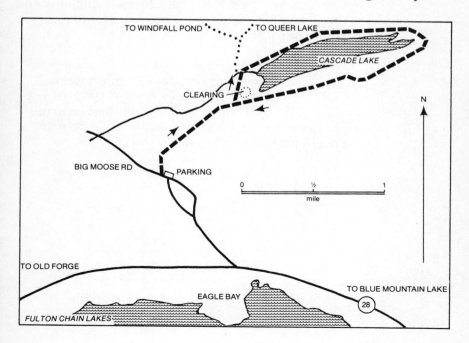

not take the trouble to accumulate enough fine wood. The flames from the fine wood must endure until the larger wood, the broom handles and the baseball bats, have really caught fire. There is usually a lot of moisture in wood taken from the winter forest, even though it looks dry, so the ignition time is longer than you might expect. It is not unusual to have the first load of tinder burn itself out before the heavier wood is fully ignited. You have to keep poking small sticks through the mass of larger wood, placing it where the flames seem to be the hottest.

The time and labor to get a really roaring campfire going in winter is considerable, so if you start to feel cold, you will be a lot colder before you feel any significant warmth from a fire. Make your first attempt on a warm day. Extra clothing, a sit-upon and tarp, and a thermos of hot tea are much better insurance against the cold chills.

This book does not purport to be a text on winter outdoor living or winter survival; this information should be sought between other covers. Savvy in back-country outdoor living makes an important contribution to your overall enjoyment, and lots of good reading on this topic is available and worthwhile.

19 Inlet to South Shore Road

Distance: 7 miles (one-way)
Maps: USGS 15' Old Forge; USGS 15' Big Moose
Groomed trails and wilderness skiing; easy terrain

After World War II, Walter Schmid, an enterprising cabinet maker and wood worker from the Black Forest of Germany, decided to try his luck in the United States. He eventually settled in the tiny hamlet of Inlet. In his youth, he had been a champion *langlaufer in der Schwartzwald* (cross-country ski racer in the Black Forest). When he became aware that Nordic skiing was coming of age, he was one of the early promoters of the sport in this part of the Adirondacks. He leased land across the road from his house, constructed a network of ski trails, and established one of the first Adirondack ski touring centers.

Time passed, and much of the land containing his trail system was sold to the State of New York by its owner. As a result the state acquired a ready-made and elaborate ski trail network. The center also offers rentals, instruction, supplies, and equipment. Because so much of the network is now on state land, no trail fee is charged. The grooming costs are defrayed as part of the town of Inlet's winter sports promotion program.

The State also maintains a public campsite at Limekiln Lake just to the south of this area. Old logging roads that went back in the woods behind this campsite crossed a section of private land and emerged at South Shore Road, which runs along the shore of the Fulton Chain of Lakes. Once the state had negotiated for public access over the private lands, a few connections were all that were required to connect the trail system built by Walter Schmid with the Limekiln Lake-South Shore Road trail. As a result, you can start at the Inlet Ski Touring Center, ski as much as you like on the center's trails, and then go 4½ miles through the woods and come out on South Shore Road. From here it is 4 miles back to the Inlet Ski Touring Center, by road, so we recommend that you park a second car here where you emerge from the woods.

Stopping by the big rock on the Inlet Ski Touring Center trail

The route described starts at the Inlet Ski Touring
Center, makes its way generally around the base of a
height-of-land, and then joins the state trail, coming
out on South Shore Road. There are, however, a
number of other interesting possibilities to be derived
from this assemblage. If your party has two cars, you
can park car one at the exit of the trail, drive car two
back to the center, ski over Walter Schmid's trails, pick
up the state trail, and ski back to car one, a seven-mile
jaunt. If you want a fourteen miler, with a place to come
in out of the cold at the halfway point, you can make
the trip by starting at South Shore Road and ski to the
center and back to your car. The Inlet Ski Touring
Center has no food service as yet, but there are several
restaurants in Inlet, ¼ mile up the road.

To reach the parking area at the tour's start, take NY
28 to Inlet and in the middle of town turn south on
South Shore Road. The road will veer to the right, and
about .2 mile from NY 28 you will see the Inlet Ski
Touring Center on your right. Check to inquire about
local conditions and to pick up a detailed map for the
trails maintained by the center.

To drive to the western terminus of the state trail
where it comes out on South Shore Road, start at the
touring center and continue west on South Shore
Road for 4 miles to a Y-fork. South Shore Road
continues to the left. One-half mile beyond this
intersection there is a parking lot on the left-hand side
of the road with a signboard indicating the "X-C Trail
to Limekiln Lake Public Campsite." This signboard
does not mention the ski touring center. This end of
the trail is also an access route to a private camp leased
from the Adirondack League Club. At times, the leasees
use snowmobiles to gain access to this camp, so do not
be disturbed if you encounter snowmobile tracks near
South Shore Road.

Starting now at the center, cross the road and enter
the woods on a short entrance trail. A large number of
trails diverge from a common point; take Trail #6 to the
left. It will shortly pass just below a huge boulder. Just
beyond, a number of trails crisscross, but pass
through this intersection, keeping on Trail #6, which
goes around the base of a height-of-land. (If you wish
more adventure in your skiing, the touring center
maintains a number of other routes that climb this
rise and then drop down the other side. Some of them
are zippy. These will eventually pick up Trail #6 again.
It is about 1½ miles to the junction with the state trail,
which is marked with yellow disks showing the figure
of a skier. Once on the state trail, it is clear sailing for
the next 4½ miles to South Shore Road.

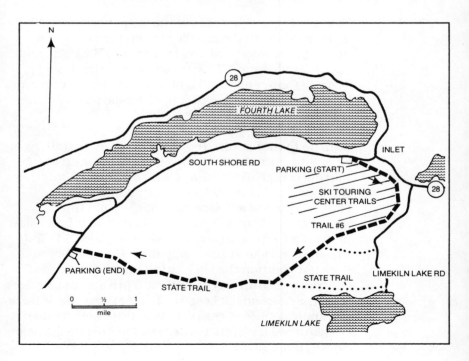

20 Truck Trail to Big Otter Lake

Distance: 16 miles
Map: USGS 15' McKeever
Easy; two hills near start

The term "truck trail" refers to the one-lane roads built by the Department of Environmental Conservation (DEC) in the Adirondack Forest Preserve and used for administrative purposes. They have just the right width and grades for ski touring.

A whole system of truck trails were built in the Forest Preserve in the late 1930s under enabling legislation that specified that only motor vehicles on official duties would be permitted on these roads. This restriction made their construction compatible with the State constitution, which requires that "the lands of the Forest Preserve be forever kept as wild forest lands."

Snowmobiles became popular in this country in the middle 1960s at a time when it seemed that no one had heard of cross-country skiing. Purchase of a snowmobile was treated then as a license to ride over snow like a boat on water; the machines went everywhere. The pioneer cross-country skiers invoked this legislation to keep the truck trails closed to the snow machines. The Big Otter Lake truck trail was one of the first ski touring routes to be discovered and has had time to become popular.

By 1968, the abuses of unrestricted snowmobile riding reached the point where further restrictions became

necessary. The new policy allowed snowmobile use on
Forest Preserve land only on those trails and routes
specifically designated and marked for such use. In
1972, the Forest Preserve lands were further designated as Wilderness, Primitive, and Wild Forest, with
the formally designated wilderness areas being completely closed to snow vehicles. The western boundary
of the Ha-de-ron-dah Wilderness area, which you will
be skiing through on this truck trail, is at Big Otter
Lake, so if you get this far, you will encounter a system
of snowmobile trails that utilize the Wild Forest Land
further to the west.

It takes a hardy skier to go all the way to Big Otter Lake
at the far end of this truck trail and return the same
day, but shorter trips going only part of the distance
are just as enjoyable. It has been a popular ski route in
the Adirondacks for some time, and there is a good

Indian Lake Brook from the truck trail

chance that you will find the tracks of other skiers, which will ease your work of breaking trail.

The truck trail to Big Otter Lake leaves NY 28 at Thendara, just south of Old Forge. From Utica take NY 12 north to the junction of NY 28 at Alder Creek, and then follow NY 28 to Thendara. Just before a railroad underpass, turn left onto a dirt road, which ends in about .5 mile at a small parking lot.

For the first few hundred feet the truck trail runs concurrently with a snowmobile trail maintained by the town of Webb. The snowmobile tracks continue due north when the ski trail breaks off to the left on an upgrade. The junction here is well marked. On the return trip use caution as you ski downhill into this intersection because the snowmobile traffic can be heavy at times.

Just beyond the top of this first rise, you will enter the Ha-de-ron-dah Wilderness Area, whose boundary is marked with a motor vehicle barrier. A series of ups and downs follows, ending in a downhill run that carries you out into the meadows of Indian Brook. Winter rambles along the banks of this waterway are delightful.

Just beyond the Indian Brook crossing you will reach signboards giving distances along the truck trail. A sign pointing in the direction you have just come gives the distance to Thendara as 2 miles. This is the distance into town; you have actually skied only 1½ miles from the parking lot.

The trail to Otter Lake now starts up a long, slow, even grade over a shoulder of Moose River Mountain. Three miles from the start, or 1½ miles from the signboards, the trail starts to descend; the slope is easy at first, but

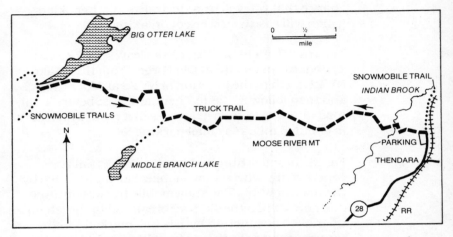

steeper near the bottom. From here on, however, the trail is more level. You climb over a small knoll at 5 miles and pass a side trail to Middle Branch and Middle Settlement lakes at 6½ miles. This side trail is rough, steep, and hard to follow.

At 7 miles you enter an open meadow. The trail is now close to and running parallel to the shore of Big Otter Lake. One mile farther on the truck trail terminates at an unplowed road coming in from the west that the DEC has officially designated as a snowmobile trail.

Almost all the Ha-de-ron-dah Wilderness Area was badly burned in the great forest fires of the late nineteenth and early twentieth centuries. These fires were usually started by sparks from wood-burning locomotives on the railroad and were further fueled by accumulations of slash left by loggers. Some of these burns damaged the soil so extensively that growth is still stunted. In summer you can discover huge charred stumps that indicate the size of the trees that stood on this land before it was logged.

21 Buck Hill State Forest

Distance: 4 miles
Maps: USGS 7.5' North Western; USGS 7.5' Boonville
Very easy grades; recommended for beginners

Buck Hill is an elongated rise with very steep sides but
a generally flat top—it's shaped somewhat like a hot-
dog roll. It is one of the state reforestation areas, and,
as an administrative aid, truck trails (single-lane
gravel roads) have been built through it. Because of the
steep side slopes, these roads cannot run straight to
the summit and over it; instead they spiral up to
produce a very even and gentle grade. The highest
point on top of Buck Hill is less than ¼ mile from the
start, air-line, but it takes 1 2/3 miles to reach it by
truck trail, with a total elevation gain of 300 vertical
feet. The grade is one that can be climbed with the
greatest of ease, and on the descent skis on fast snow
will just slide along at an even pace.

Buck Hill has many other features that make it
attractive. The site is only some twenty-five miles from
the New York State Thruway (I-90) at Utica and about
forty miles from Syracuse. Located about ten miles
almost due south of Boonville and at an elevation of
1,200 to 1,000 feet, it receives the heavy snowfalls
typical of the Tug Hill Plateau area and consequently
has a long snow season. Even better, the truck trail
requires a minimum of snow cover to make it skiable,
so here is the place for an early season or late season
ski trip.

If you are approaching from the south, take NY 46
north from Rome past the Delta Reservoir State Park
and the hamlet of North Western. Twelve miles from
Rome and less than .5 mile beyond North Western you
cross a cast cement bridge. Directly beyond, the road
forks. Bear right, uphill. The sign at the corner will
indicate Alder Creek Road. If you are approaching from
the north on NY 46 this intersection is 13 miles by
road from Booneville, and the turnoff will be a sharp
hairpin bend to the left. Within a mile of leaving NY 46
you will see steep ground on your left, and 1.4 miles

A herd of deer is an extraordinary sight

from the intersection you will see the truck trail coming in from the left. There is a pole here to support a large signboard for the Buck Hill State Forest, but the sign that normally hangs there may be taken in for the winter. Park along the side of the road.

The road starts off in a southwest direction and proceeds to spiral its way up Buck Hill. As you go around the first bend, views to the valley to the south will start to open up through the hardwoods. Did you know that the headwaters of the Mohawk River would be beneath you here? The popular conception is that the Mohawk is an east-west river that runs along the Barge Canal for most of its length. Not so. And while we are talking about water, did you see evidence of the old canal and the locks that ran more or less alongside NY 46 as you approached the trail's start? After the success of the Erie Canal in 1820, New York State went canal crazy and built them everywhere. This particular canal, the Black River Canal, went from Rome to Carthage.

The truck trail has now swung around so you are heading due north. To your right is a steep slope with very open hardwoods. If you aspire to do telemarks in powder snow, here is the chance to do some glade skiing. In 1 mile you reach the first of two trail junctions. You can bear uphill to the right now, or continue a short distance to the second and then bear right. The two routes converge in ¼ mile; the first is steeper than the second. The way left at the second junction dead-ends in a stand of red pines.

We propose that you climb the farther of the right-hand forks. As you near the top of the ridge, you ski through a stand of small white pines. To the left a side road runs along a row of big maple trees; we have never explored this route, but the avenue of maples suggests that it was once a farm lane.

Five hundred feet farther you come to a T-junction where there is a planting of larch. The larch is a coniferous tree that loses its needles in winter, presenting a yellowish brown appearance. We've dubbed this spot "Larch Corner."

Now bear left, or north; shortly the truck trail divides. The two routes rejoin later on, but the left-hand or upper road continues more or less level and has the

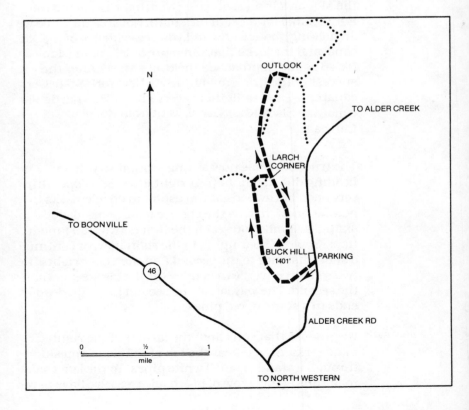

better outlooks. The best views over the rolling country to the east are to be had where this road turns to the right and drops downhill to meet the lower road again.

You now will have gone 2 miles and we suggest you turn around here. On the way back you will see the top of Buck Hill as a prominent height-of-land on the horizon. Make this your next objective. When you come to Larch Corner again, ski straight ahead. The hill's highest point is wooded so there are no outstanding views, but you have a feeling of satisfaction in having gone to the top nonetheless.

From here back to the car, you can almost stand still and let your skis simply move you along. Once in awhile you will need a double-pole thrust to keep up the momentum. And if you stride hard, you will feel like you're wearing seven-league boots. It is only ½ mile back to Larch Corner, where you turn left and shortly come to the junction of the two short trails that come together again at the slope's bottom. These are the only significant hills on this tour. Remember, the one to the left is the steeper. Take your pick and shove off. If the snow is fast, you will not stop moving until you arrive at the parking lot.

Buck Hill is well named. We have seen more deer tracks in and around this site than at almost any other spot in this book. If you go carefully and quietly, you might see a deer or two yourself.

22 Lesser Wilderness State Forest

Distance: 7 miles
Map: USGS 7.5' Glenfield
Easy terrain; skiing from November to May

In the early days of New York, two regions were considered too formidable and inhospitable by settlers. The vast Adirondack region was known as the Greater Wilderness, while the Tug Hill Plateau just east of Lake Ontario was called the Lesser Wilderness. When a tract of land in this area was acquired by the state for reforestation and multiple-use purposes, it was given the name from long ago, the Lesser Wilderness State Forest. The greatest snowfall in the Tug Hill area falls about a mile away from this forest, near Gomer Hill, the plateau's highest point of land. The skiing season here can start in early November and last into May.

The ground on top of the plateau is gently rolling, and the grades on this tour are easy. While the recommended tour takes full advantage of the distance opportunities and thus develops a 7-mile route, unplowed town roads pass through the area, intersecting the trail so that shorter trips can be arranged.

Because your approach is through the Black River Valley there is less chance of encountering a heavy and sudden lake effect snowstorm than if you were driving on the top of the Tug Hill Plateau. Starting from the village of Turin, head north on NY 26 for 2.3 miles and turn left onto Carpenter Road. (This junction is .6 mile south of Houseville.) A signboard here points to the Lesser Wilderness Ski Trail. In .4 mile you will pass Jim Wright's Nordic Gnome Ski Shop, a good source of local information. Just beyond, the road turns left through a farmyard. Four-tenths of a mile farther it makes a right-hand hairpin turn and goes up a short, steep hill. It is well to shift into a lower gear before you come to this rise. The trailhead at Seymour Road, an unplowed town road at the top of the hill, is marked with a sign on the left-hand side. Continue on about 100 feet until the ground levels off and park on the side of the road.

Edging closer for a look at Mill Creek in the Lesser Wilderness State Forest

The trail layout consists of two loops: the West Loop and the Snow Ridge Loop. You will ski the West Loop, about 3½ miles around, first. The Snow Ridge Loop, which you reach second, is only slightly longer than 1 mile. The two are joined by a trail about ¼ mile long. A glance at the map will fix these arrangements in your mind. These directions will have you take the loops clockwise so your departure from Seymour Road, which you follow at first, will be a left-hand turn.

As you go up unplowed Seymour Road there will be an open field to the left and a pine plantation to the right. The trees look stunted: this is deliberate. These trees are used to harvest pine cones to obtain seed for other reforestation projects. The trees are pruned to a shape to make pine cone harvesting easier. As you continue to gain altitude, views will open up across the field to the valley of the Black River and into the western Adirondacks. One-half mile from the start, you will reach a signboard showing where the West Loop comes in from the right, or west. This is where you will finally emerge after you have traversed the complete trail system. Keep on Seymour road another 1/10 mile. The field to the left terminates in some low scrub growth, while Seymour Road just ahead looks low and marshy.

Bear left here; the first leg of the West Loop is called Jack's Track, but there is no signboard at this corner. The trail goes between a line of fenceposts and the edge of the scrub and is marked with daubs of yellow paint on the trees and some strips of flagging tape. Shortly you leave behind the completely open farm field you have had on your left-hand side since the start of the trip and pass into a reverted field, dotted with thorn-apple and white pine. As you enter this area, the trail turns left for a second time. Watch for yellow disk trail markers and flagging tape when crossing this short

section. The trail then enters plantation pines, and the
rest of the Jack's Track is in the forest.

The pines are soon left behind in favor of hardwoods.
There is a pleasant downgrade, and shortly a set of
signboards will come into view that tell you you have
come from Seymour Road via Jack's Track and that the
Snow Ridge Loop is straight ahead. The fork to the
right, called the Mill Creek Trail, is the return leg of the

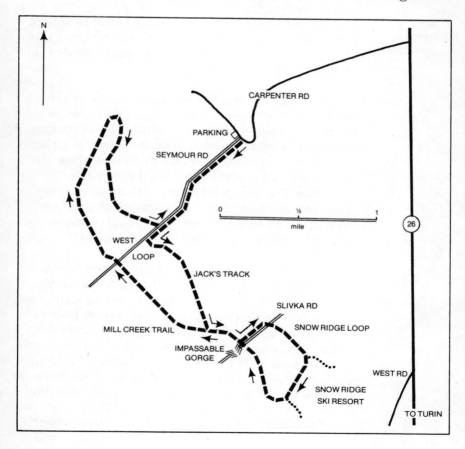

West Loop you will pick up later in the day. Another signboard also directs you to Slivka Road, an abandoned town road that the Snow Ridge Loop utilizes for a short distance.

You now will ski down some easy grades, pass through an open area and shortly come upon Slivka Road. The sign here is novel: two ski tips have been nailed to a post and painted "Slivka Road." Think of Slivka Road as a name for a trail junction, not a highway. True, you can see the remains of an abandoned town road here, but it doesn't go anyplace. A very short stretch of this old road has been made part of the next section of ski trail, the Snow Ridge Loop.

The Snow Ridge Loop is named for the nearby private ski area of that name, whose boundaries come very close to the trail you will be traveling. Three connectors to the private ski area branch off the Snow Ridge Loop. You will not inadvertently end up on one of these if you remember that you will be skiing the loop in a clockwise direction, which means that you will stay with the right-hand fork every time a trail junction presents itself. In every case, the trail you want will be marked with the yellow trail disks of the DEC.

Take a left turn on Slivka Road heading northeast, and in 1/10 mile take a right turn off the road, following the DEC trail markers. You will be traveling southeast. The second turnoff will present itself ¼ mile from Slivka Road, where the Snow Ridge Loop heads almost due south. You pass the third turnoff within another ¼ mile. This turnoff heads to the southeast, while your trail heads to the west. Once past this you are home free. You complete the Snow Ridge Loop by returning to Slivka Road, then retrace your steps to the signboards on the West Loop, and take what is now the right-hand fork leading up the Mill Creek Trail. This is the most scenic part of the route. The stream flows in the early winter and late spring, winding and turning in a deep gorge to your left.

There have been a lot of small downhill sections up to this point and these must be climbed in a gentle grade to reach Seymour Road again. If you wish to cut your trip short, take a right-hand turn here. The start of Jack's Track, where you first left Seymour Road, is only ¼ mile to the north of here.

Continuing across Seymour Road on the West Loop, you climb some barely perceptible grades. The trail will veer more to the northwest. About 1 mile from the road crossing, it swings around a hairpin loop and heads back. The accumulation of these imperceptible climbs now will pay off in a pleasant downhill ride. Seymour Road comes quickly.

The best views of the trip are found on the way back to the car. The valley of the Black River is spread out before you. On a clear day Lowville is seen to the left, and beyond it, the western slopes of the Adirondacks.

23 Whetstone Gulf

Distance: 4 miles
Maps: USGS 7.5' Glenfield; park map
Very easy, then difficult skiing; outstanding gorge

There are many ravines and gorges in New York but none with such extreme depth and narrowness as Whetstone Gulf, located on the eastern edge of the Tug Hill Plateau. Add a setting of a state park with a heated lodge, warm-up trails near the parking lot, and park rangers who also understand cross-country skiing, and you have an unbeatable combination.

The bedrock of the Tug Hill Plateau is a compressed shale, which is less resistant to water erosion than most rocks, so that streams can cut valleys downward through it faster than they can cut sideways. The Tug Hill Plateau region is characterized by twelve such narrow deep gorges, locally known as "gulfs," of which Whetstone Gulf is an outstanding example. At the point where it emerges from the steep-faced eastern edge of the plateau the gulf floor is perhaps two hundred feet wide. As you make your way up this chasm, the valley beomes narrower and the side walls steeper. In the last ½ mile, the side walls are so nearly vertical that no vegetation can hang on, and at the falls all the way in, they are only five to six feet apart.

Near the entrance the valley floor is sufficiently wide that the Thousand Islands State Park Commission has been able to develop a good, wide trail that extends ¾ mile into the gulf. This much of the tour is over level or

slightly sloping grades and is within the skiing ability
of almost anyone. Beyond the ¾-mile mark, the nature
of the gorge can make skiing difficult. The south-
facing wall warms in the sunshine and cools off at
night, and the resulting hot-cool cycle of summer and
freeze-thaw action of winter continually loosen
material, which sifts down to the valley floor. This
action occurs more frequently at certain points, giving
rise to large cone-shaped fans of detritus composed of
loose shale rock in summer and snow and ice in
winter. The snow texture in these fans is much firmer
and harder than that of the normal winter snow in the
valley bottom, and this can present difficulty. Usually it
is possible to cross the creek on a snow bridge to go
around such formations, but at times, they form formidable obstacles where you have to side-step up one
slope and ski down the other. This can be a tricky
operation with changing snow textures, which is why
the upper section of the gorge is rated difficult.

Snow sifting into Whetstone Gulf

A park ranger skis up the gulf frequently to inspect the route and advise visitors of what to expect. Good skiing conditions are normally expected from the first week of January through the second week in February. During this period the Whetstone Creek is frozen and very little meltwater is expected. The snow in the bottom accumulates to great depths, so when you can see the stream at all it may be ten to fifteen feet below you. Also, in deep midwinter the freeze-thaw action on the side walls is minimal. After the middle of February the conditions in the bottom are entirely dependent on the melt-and-freeze history of the winter. We visited the area in the first week of March just after an unexpected thaw had produced a flood of such proportions that the park bridges at the bottom were washed out.

In the event that you arrive when this tour is not suitable, try one of the other ski touring routes available; a trail around the rim of Whetstone Gulf also exists, where good snow conditions should persist well into April. This tour is not described here, but maps and directions for it can be obtained at the lodge. In addition, summer campsite roads near the lodge are utilized as short warm-up ski trails. You can test your wax in the few minutes it takes to breeze around these loops.

The Whetstone Gulf State Park is located off NY 26 about 4 miles north of Turin. Route NY 26 has been renumbered and is shown as NY 12D on older road maps. There is a large sign on NY 26 opposite the park entrance. As you enter you will pass a registration booth and some administration buildings. The booth is not manned in winter, but all visitors are asked to sign in and out as a safety measure. The visitor parking area and the lodge are about 500 feet straight ahead.

You can look into the bottom portion of the gulf from
the lodge and sense the height of the side slopes. Start
your tour behind the lodge and cross the brook on a
footbridge. The water will now be on your left. The first
½ mile is double-width trail that leads into a summer
picnic area. Beyond this point the sides of the canyon
start to close in and the trail narrows to footpath
width. In summer the trail is close to Whetstone Creek,
but in winter the Tug Hill snowfalls and the
continuous shedding of snow from the steep upper
slopes elevates the track, so you may be skiing ten or
fifteen feet above the water. The trail is easy for the
first ¾ mile or so. Beyond this point the cone-shaped
fans may present technical skiing problems. This
point is marked with a sign that park rangers move up
or down the valley according to conditions.

Here you may become aware of a silence so intense as
to be deafening. The wind may be howling on top, but
in the depth of this chasm, not a whisper will
penetrate. The soft snow on the side walls soaks up all
the sound. Your breathing, and even your heartbeat,
become intrusive. You hardly dare speak to your com-
panions, and if you do, it is likely to be in hushed tones.

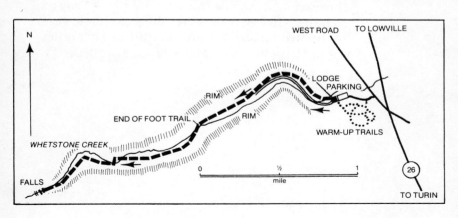

The next ¾ mile is usually a pleasant journey, moving from one side of the creek to the other to avoid the locally steep side walls that may crowd you too close to the creek's edge. When you have gone 1½ miles the vegetation on the side walls will become noticeably more sparse and the appearance of the gulf more alpine. Now the track must rely entirely on the snow bridges over the frozen stream. At the 2-mile mark the walls of the chasm are too steep to retain any growth. While jet-black shale may appear far above you, the walls at the bottom will be stark white. As you go around bends in the valley, they appear to merge in a continuous wall of whiteness. The sky is a mere slot overhead. Confined in this whiteness you feel totally alone, totally cut off from the world. It is an eerie experience.

The ultimate in this trip is to be able to approach the falls at the upper end through a slit so narrow that you can touch both walls with your finger tips. The falls themselves corkscrew down through a flume to the left and then plunge through a hole in the snow into a pool beneath.

Those who have made this trip many times say that each time they go in, it is ever different but always impressive. It is truly a journey into another other world, a penetration into the caverns of silence.

24 Jefferson County Forest

Distance: 3¼ miles
Map: USGS 7.5' Barnes Corners
Easy grades; two open shelters, forest variety

In the late 1970s a number of Federal programs gave financial assistance to local community improvement projects. In Tug Hill areas this source of funding was often used to develop cross-country ski trails. This particular trail was built by the Youth Conservation Corps (YCC) in the summer of 1978. Jefferson County Forest is located about twenty-five miles southeast of Watertown and seventy miles from Syracuse. At an elevation of 1,400 feet, it receives the heavy snowfalls typical of the western side of the Tug Hill Plateau, so it normally provides skiing from November through April.

As is the case in all Tug Hill locations, those coming into the area must be wary of the Lake Ontario snow-storms. Be sure to read the description of these storms and the precautions to be taken in the Introduction to this guide.

Jefferson County Forest is public land owned and managed by the Jefferson County Soil and Water Conservation District. Unlike most areas mentioned in this book, it is not part of the landholdings of the New York State Department of Environmental Conservation (DEC).

The only highway across the Tug Hill Plateau is NY 177 from Adams Center to Lowville. To some extent this road divides the area into productive and wilderness zones. There is farming to the north of NY 177, but to the south the land is swampy and poorly drained. Looking at your road map you will see a large blank spot lying generally to the south of NY 177. This is the truly desolate part of the Tug Hill Plateau, and this trail lies right on the edge of it.

The swampy terrain is an advantage in ski trail design. Whereas most of the routes in this book are entirely forested, this one has almost the appearance of a Japanese landscape as it goes from low scrub pines to open pool-like areas and back again. Parts of the trail pass through impressive pine glades and parts through some nice hardwood stands. The YCC has also

Because of the extraordinary snow depths, the shelter in Jefferson County Forest stands several feet off the ground

built two open shelters with floors more than four feet off the ground that are reached by a flight of steps. As the snows accumulate to full depth, it is more likely that you will step down into these shelters than climb up. The hills are easy ups and downs that will not give beginners any problems.

The starting point for driving directions is the junction of NY 178 with the through route across the plateau, NY 177. This junction is 9 miles from Adams Center on the west and 19 miles from Lowville on the east. Turn south on NY 178. In 1.9 miles you will come to Loomis Road, where a sign gives the names of the YCC workers who built this trail. You can start here, but as this connecting route has steep grades the recommended entrance is on the other side of Jefferson County Forest. You come into the town of Worth 2.5 miles from NY 177. Worth is little more than a triangular road intersection. Take the unmarked left-hand turn at the Town of Worth garage. This road is actually Jefferson Co. #96. Continuing along the county road for 1.1 miles you will come to an intersection by a red barn, a big silo, and a white house. Continue straight on and cross a bridge: within .2 mile you will arrive at the parking lot, on the left.

Here the sign, "CETA loop, 3.25 miles," refers to the Comprehensive Employment Training Act, which funded this project. The trail is marked with DEC yellow trail disks only as far as the first trail junction. You will also see blue and yellow paint on some trees; these are foresters' marks, not trail markers. Disregard them.

Starting in the woods at the parking lot, the trail will cross an open area and then take an upgrade, not too steep. The trail is very wide and well cut. There are arrows wherever a change in direction is indicated.

In ¼ mile an arrow painted on a signboard points to the left, while an old woods road goes straight. Looking at the signboard carefully you will see in light letters "Beaver Dam, Route 178 parking lot." In talking to the local forest ranger and others we learned that this trail may be improved and enlarged in the summer of 1979, so it is possible that new marking signs will be installed and other skiing opportunities will be added. For an update on trail information contact the South Jefferson Chamber of Commerce, Adams, NY 13605 (phone: 315-232-4070).

The trail now runs through some red pines, and shortly it will break into hardwoods. In about ¾ mile you will reach a stream on the left with fairly steep banks. At the time of this writing, there was an arrow here with faint lettering "Rt 178 parking lot, 1.6 miles." Looking into the valley you will see a beaver dam and its pond to the south and southeast.

The trail then assumes a direction of due north and enters a stand of impressively large red pines, all thinned out to make glades. Just ahead you will encounter the first of the two shelters built high off the ground, which will place you 8/10 mile from the start.

The trail continues north, then swings to the east and climbs somewhat. This point is about 1 mile from the beginning. A downhill section, not at all steep or difficult, follows. The trail swings around in an S-bend 1¾ miles from the start, first toward the south, then east, and then south again. Here you will find the second shelter.

From here it is 1¼ miles back to your start. The going is very pleasant without any real hills—only a slight rise and an easy descent—so there is enough variation in the terrain to provide a continuous change of pace.

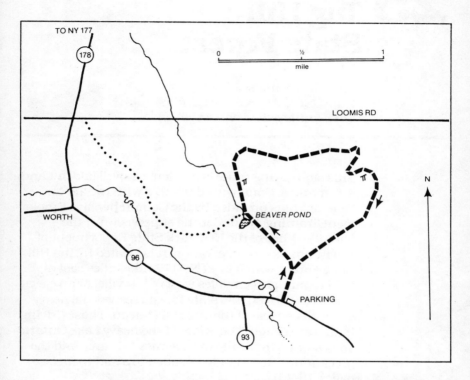

We have not described the route that comes in from the parking lot at the junction of Loomis Road and NY 178. There is one quite steep section in a hill near the beaver dam so this trail is not recommended for beginners. For those more expert, starting at this point and skiing around the loop just mentioned will develop a trip about 6 miles long.

There is also another ski touring trail in this vicinity. In the summer of 1978 the Tug Hill State Forest crew completed a ski-touring trail about four miles from here. If you are the gung-ho type that likes to cover ground, you can do both in one day. The Tug Hill tour is described on the following pages (Tour 25).

25 Tug Hill State Forest

Distance: 5 miles
Map: USGS 7.5' Barnes Corners
Easy grades; long snow season

This ski-touring route is particularly well laid out and well marked. Constructed in 1978 with the aid of Federal funds provided by the Comprehensive Employment Training Act under the supervision of the Lowville Office of the New York State Department of Environmental Conservation, it is located in Tug Hill State Forest, which is off NY 177 nine miles east of US 11 and eighteen miles west of Lowville. At an elevation of 1,400 feet, this state forest receives the heavy snowfalls typical of the Tug Hill Plateau. Those driving in this area should be aware of the heavy Lake Ontario snowstorms that can sweep across this area and the precautions that should be taken to avoid them (see pages 16-20).

The first tract of land in Tug Hill State Forest was acquired by the state in 1933 for $4 an acre as part of a program to buy up abandoned farmlands. To illustrate how the Depression destroyed land values, farmland in this area sold for $33 per acre in 1874. The forest now covers 12,000 acres—a tract of 18¾ square miles, which if square would be better than 4½ miles on a side. The trail system described here occupies only a small fraction of the total area.

While this land was acquired by the state to harvest forest products, it has never been completely cut over.

Those sales that did occur were carefully managed to remove only those trees ready for harvest or in the growing space of nearby better trees.

Inman Gulf, one of the spectacular steep-sided gulfs that characterize the Tug Hill Plateau, is nearby. A practical route from the marked ski trails to the gulf does not exist at this time, but a short side trip will be mentioned at the tour's end so that you can get a peek into it.

Coming from Lowville, on the east, head for Barnes Corners on NY 177. You will pass a sign indicating the boundary of the state forest .8 mile past Barnes Corners and another for the Jefferson-Lewis county line in 1.6 miles; at 1.8 miles a third sign, on the right-

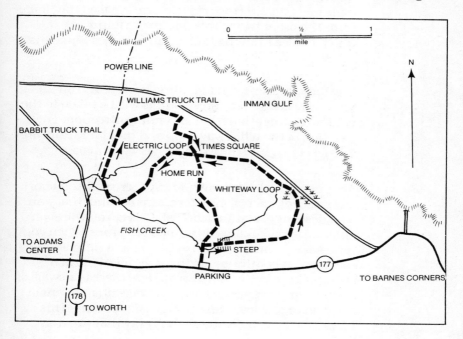

hand or north side of the road, marks the entrance to the Tug Hill State Forest ski trails. There is quite a wide opening in the forest here, while back from the road 100 feet or so is a green-painted storage shed. Driving east, the trail is 5.5 miles east of Rodman and .7 mile east of the intersection of NY 178 and NY 177.

A large plastic-covered map of the area has been erected here at the outset, so if you have left your map at home, you can refresh your memory. The trail system is in the form of a somewhat distorted figure-eight. The point where the two halves of the figure-eight intersect is called Times Square. The loop that leaves Times Square to the left, or west, is called the Electric Loop because it passes near a high-voltage transmission line. The trail from the parking area that leads most directly to Times Square is called the Home Run. The other half of this part of the figure-eight, which circles from the Home Run to Times Square is called the Whiteway Loop.

The tour we selected using these trails starts on the Whiteway Loop so the steeper hills will be taken in the climbing rather than the descending direction. The junction of the Whiteway Loop and the Home Run, only 700 feet or so into the woods, is very well marked.

About ¼ mile along the Whiteway there will be a short steep ascent, then a short level stretch, and finally an easy descent to a branch of Fish Creek. You will soon enter an area of tall, well-thinned red pines. When you have gone 2/3 mile the trail will bend at a right angle to the north. It continues north for 1/3 mile and then swings to the left, or northwest. Here there is a swale of swampy growth, and you can see the embankment of the Williams Truck Trail through the opening. This truck trail is actually the old highway that ran from

Barnes Corners west across the plateau until the
present NY 177 was built. Proceeding northwest, you
come to a second swamp where the truck trail again
comes into view, this time farther in the distance.
Shortly beyond this, or at about the 1½-mile point, the
trail swings to the west. It brings you to Times Square
at 1¾ miles. The intersection is very well marked with
signs noting various distances.

We propose that you now go around the Electric Loop
in a clockwise direction. When you get to the
westernmost stretch of this trail, you may opt to leave
the deep white pine growth and ski under the
transmisssion line where you will be in the sun, and it
is more pleasant to have the sun at your back rather
than in your face so you don't have to take the glare off
the snow. The power line parallels the trail for ½ mile.
When the ground starts to tilt downhill, that is your
signal to head back into the woods to pick up the trail
again. About 1/3 mile from the point where the trail
turns right, or east, from the transmission line, the
trail zigzags somewhat. When you have reached this
spot you are less than ¼ mile from Times Square. The
Home Run back to the start will require a right-hand
turn at that junction and a trip of 1 mile.

Perhaps you wish to look down into Inman Gulf.
Driving east towards Barnes Corners on NY 177, note
on your right where the Williams Truck Trail comes out
on the highway. Drive .2 mile beyond and at the edge of
a patch of woods, look for an unplowed road leaving to
the left, or north. This road is less than .2 mile long and
dead-ends at the brink of the gulf. A highway stop sign
marks the end.

If you have time you may wish to try another ski tour
in this vicinity. Tour 24, in Jefferson County Forest, is
only four miles away.

Guidebooks from New Hampshire Publishing Company

Written for people of all ages and experience, these highly popular and carefully prepared books feature detailed trail directions, notes on points of interest, sketch maps, and photographs.

For cross-country skiers—

25 Ski Tours in the Green Mountains
Fords. $4.95

25 Ski Tours in Western Massachusetts
Frado et al. $4.95

25 Ski Tours in the White Mountains
Fords. $4.95

25 Ski Tours in Maine
Beiser. $5.95

25 Ski Tours in Connecticut
Wass and Alvord. $4.95

About New York State—

Discover the Adirondacks, 1
McMartin. $6.95

Discover the Adirondacks, 2
McMartin (January 1980). $6.95

25 Walks in the Finger Lakes Region
Ehling. $5.95

Other books of interest—

Fifty Hikes in Vermont
Sadliers (Revised ed. 1980). $6.95

20 Bicycle Tours in Vermont
Freidin. $5.95

Canoe Camping Vermont and New Hampshire Rivers
Schweiker. $4.95

Fifty Hikes in Central Pennsylvania
Thwaites. $6.95

Available from bookstores, sporting goods stores, or the publisher. For complete descriptions of these and other guides in the **Fifty Hikes, 25 Walks, Bicycle Tour, Canoeing,** and **Fishing** series, write: New Hampshire Publishing Company, Box 70, Somersworth, NH 03878.